SIGNS OF HIS LIGHT:

SPIRITUAL LESSONS FROM MY JOURNEY WITH CANCER

RITA CARBUHN

Signs of His Light: Spiritual Lessons from My Journey with Cancer

Cover creation courtesy of Rita Carbuhn and Ravi Verma from https://rdezines.com

Editing and formatting by Lorraine Reguly from www.WordingWell.com

Dedication

To Mother

—my best friend and role model for life—

and

To the Glory of Jesus, my Lord and Savior!

Table of Contents

A Time for Everything

*There is a time for everything and a season
for every activity under heaven:*

A time to be born and a time to die,
A time for plant and a time to uproot,
A time to kill and a time to heal,
A time to tear down and a time to build,
A time to weep and a time to laugh,
A time to mourn and a time to dance,
*A time to scatter stones and a time to gather
them,*

A time to embrace and a time to refrain,
A time to search and a time to give up,
A time to keep and a time to throw away,
A time to tear and a time to mend,
A time to be silent and a time to speak,
A time to love and a time to hate,
A time for war and a time for peace.

Ecclesiastes 3:1-8,
New International Version (NIV)

RITA CARBUHN

Preface

Throughout my struggle with cancer, I learned firsthand what it meant to walk with my Lord and Savior. I became keenly aware of how He existed in my heart. More importantly, I learned to discern His presence in my daily life. He provided valuable insight into my experience, which I called "signs." It was a simple message.

My Lord was the light on which I focused and it is because of Him that my story can be shared.

Prior to my diagnosis, I had an intense feeling I would soon embark on a journey and that something big was about to happen. I felt compelled to record my thoughts and feelings. Honestly, I was clueless but, for some reason, it seemed very important. So, I obeyed and trusted I would understand later.

Then I was diagnosed with cancer.

Suddenly, everything began to fall into place.

My daily recordings became my journal in which I could express my thoughts and feelings without judgment. Writing became a valuable outlet and I wrote poems of grief, praise, and thanksgiving. I read multiple books relating to cancer, especially those related to others' experiences with this disease. They offered support.

Music soothed my soul and renewed my strength daily. I looked for ways to relax and meditate and found prayer to be the answer! Praying carried me through my painful and weakest moments. It also strengthened my reliance on my Lord. I looked to His eternal light of hope and healing so I could move toward another tomorrow.

I am now able to share my story. It is my wish to offer you support and encouragement for your journey toward health and healing. Whether your challenge is a physical illness or some other kind of obstacle, it can be overcome by trusting the Lord. Although it may seem like an impossible task, a positive outcome is possible. However, don't be surprised if the outcome is entirely different from what you expect! There will be pain along the way but the rewards far exceed the agony. I assure you His light is waiting at the end of that long, dark tunnel!

In fact, His hand is reaching out for you right now! Grab hold! He is waiting and desperately wants you to come to Him! If you do, He will accompany you on your journey through the darkness and you will be a victor!

This book is divided into chapters which speak to the "spiritual signs" given to me. Initially, I didn't see them as signs because they seemed like ordinary life events and I honestly didn't believe God would provide me with special messages. *What do I have to offer Him? Why would He want to communicate with me in such a special way?* I assumed a sign from God would occur as a mystical transformation or vision.

Furthermore, I thought only "holy" people were given such a gift because God intended to use them in a unique way for His ministry. I didn't see myself as holy! Only in hindsight did I realize how narrow my view of God was. The fact that God would work in such small and ordinary ways to get my attention was evidence of His eagerness and great yearning to demonstrate His love. Indeed, it is His desire to walk with each of us daily.

This story is my journey of spiritual enlightenment. My eyes were opened so I could really "see" Him and invite Him wholly into my heart forever. It is my sincere wish for your eyes and heart to be opened, too!

RITA CARBUHN

THE 1st SIGN: THE GRAND AM SLAM

"For I know the plans I have for you" declares the Lord, "plans to prosper you and not to harm you, plans to give you hope and a future." (Jeremiah 29:11, NIV)

My journey began on a cold and windy September day. As I arrived at the hospital where I worked and parked the car, my mind was already focused on the day's goals. I hurriedly got out of my car (a Grand Am) and slammed the door shut… only to realize my right breast was caught in the car door! Yes, it was actually squashed in the locked door—a pretty unbelievable feat!

Even to this day, I cannot comprehend how it happened, but I managed to locate the keys in my purse, unlock the door, and extricate myself from a very awkward and painful situation. Yes, the pain was excruciating! I fell to my knees in the parking lot and gasped for air. Tears streamed down my face, but the cold wind dried them instantly. I struggled to regain my composure and looked for help, but there was no one around.

After twenty minutes, the pain subsided enough to pull myself together and walk into the hospital. As much as I needed help, I was thankful no one had witnessed my accident. I was very embarrassed with what had occurred.

For weeks afterward, I had a black and blue right breast. The bruise covered my entire right side, from the axillary area to my waist, and from the midpoint of my sternum to the midpoint of my back. Every time I looked at myself, the whole scene replayed itself in my mind and I felt incredibly foolish! I couldn't understand how getting my breast caught in the door was possible! Perhaps it would have made more sense if I had been large-busted, but I'm not.

Whenever I told my friends about what happened, they winced at the thought and exclaimed, "Eweh!" Next came the question, "How did you do THAT?" This question was always accompanied by a look of utter disbelief. The final reaction was a broad smile followed with laughter—yes, full-out peals of laughter! This set of reactions occurred every time I told someone about my incident. Initially, it made me angry and I thought people were cruel and insensitive. However, I came to realize it was an odd chain of events and part of it, at least, was quite comical! Nonetheless, I was totally baffled. What words could explain something I didn't understand?

Although I had been faithful in completing monthly breast self-exams, I stopped because they hurt. My right breast was so tender that even the smallest touch was extraordinarily painful. For many weeks, I wore a cotton camisole because a bra created too much pressure. Gradually, the pain and bruises disappeared. Before long, I actually forgot about the incident. There were too many other demands at work that required my attention. Besides, that incident was now behind me. I thought it was over.

In late October, during my annual exam, my gynecologist calmly announced, "You have a lump in your breast." I was totally taken off-guard. I looked at her in complete shock and had to admit, I was unaware of it. She had me palpate it and, to my surprise, it was a large lump that couldn't be missed.

A sense of dread came over me. *This cannot be happening. How could such a large lump have developed so quickly?* Only a month earlier, my annual mammogram had shown nothing, so I was truly puzzled. In the back of mind was the immediate thought of cancer. I knew if a lump had not been found earlier and now one was this large, it was likely cancer. Despite having no family history of breast cancer, I knew my risk was higher because I was in my forties and didn't have any pregnancies during my lifetime.

Mostly, I was confused why I had not discovered the lump myself. By the time I left the office, I felt numb. Strangely enough, not once did I recall the car door incident. However, when I slammed the door shut in my garage at home, it all came rushing back.

Of course, I have a lump—it has to be a hematoma—a blood clot! I called the office immediately to tell the doctor, but she referred me to a surgeon anyway, for a second opinion.

My surgeon maintained his composure rather well when I explained what had now become known as "the Grand Am slam."

He did, however, ask the inevitable question, "Now, just exactly how did you do that?"

Feeling exasperated, I answered, "It really doesn't matter. I just did it." I detected a faint smile on his lips, as if he couldn't believe what he was hearing, but he never openly laughed like others did.

Only much later in our relationship did he confess he was fighting with himself not to smile or laugh. I appreciated his honesty. He agreed my assessment might be right. We both decided to monitor it for the next month to see if it would decrease in size. If not, a biopsy would be needed.

My mind was at ease with the "wait and see" outcome even though it didn't offer a final resolution. I was so sure my lump was a hematoma that I honestly believed the referral to a surgeon was unnecessary. I turned my attention to a laparotomy and possible hysterectomy that had been scheduled several months earlier. This was a surgery that my gynecologist and I had agreed upon in a previous appointment.

Over the years, I had experienced severe menstrual cramping and excessive bleeding. I had literally begged my physicians for relief. I don't think they really understood the amount of pain and discomfort I experienced daily. They wouldn't consider a permanent surgical option, but were content to perform yet another procedure or prescribe a different medication. I had been through a D&C, a colposcopy, several uterine biopsies, vaginal ultrasounds, frozen sections, and an endless variety of medications to relieve my symptoms.

Nothing worked. What I got in return was weight gain (30 pounds in five months!) and mood swings from the hormones.

Despite all of this, the painful and difficult periods continued every two weeks! I hit the end of my rope six months earlier and was at the point of looking for a permanent solution.

This gynecologist was new. During my first appointment, she asked why I had not obtained a hysterectomy yet. I was so thankful she understood my dilemma and agony. We discussed the fact that I would never be able to have children, which was something I had already accepted. All I desired was relief from my pain! However, when we were doing the work-up prior to my surgery, an ultrasound revealed that my left ovary was a solid mass. This discovery frightened me.

Oh, my gosh, not more cancer?

The gynecologist told me she didn't think it was cancerous, but we both realized the answer would be revealed in the surgery. In the meantime, I had a calm and soothing voice telling me I would be okay. I believed it was the Holy Spirit urging me to rest in Him.

Thankfully, all turned out well. There was no cancer, but I did have severe endometriosis and adenomyosis. My left ovary had shriveled to nothing and the right one was dysfunctional, at best. I would never have become pregnant, even if I tried.

After my surgery and recovery, I was in high spirits. For the first time in my adult life, I felt no pain and life was good. I thought the next year was going to be fantastic!

My follow-up appointment with my surgeon was in February. However, because I was busy at work, I missed it. By the time I could arrange another one, it was the end of March.

During that visit, he confirmed what I already knew—my lump had not decreased! I felt it daily, even though I tried to deny it! It's funny what our minds do even though, as a nurse, I knew better!

Without further hesitation, a biopsy and possible lumpectomy were scheduled for early April. My anxiety erupted once again. I had been so sure it was a hematoma, but I was wrong. The evidence was leaning in another direction and I was truly frightened at the prospect! This was when the strange "gut feeling" emerged about embarking on a journey.

What does this mean? Is this the Holy Spirit speaking? Or is it my own anxiety?

What bothered me was my inability to dissipate my sense of overwhelming fear. It disrupted my normal positive attitude and outlook on life.

As time passed, my anxiety began to increase on a daily basis and I wondered if I was losing my mind.

When my surgeon entered the operating room that April morning, I blurted out, "What if this is cancer? We haven't talked about that."

He replied, "Let's just do the surgery and see what it looks like. We will talk later."

He looked uncomfortable with my question and I wasn't satisfied with his answer. I'm not sure what I was expecting, because neither of us knew anything, at that point. Feeling the sedative effects from my medication, I was drowsy, but he told me he would share his impressions once he saw the lump. I trusted him implicitly. Before the medication took effect, he prayed for the surgery. Calm surrounded me and I nodded off. Because of its size and appearance, the lump was removed. The surgeon's assessment was it appeared to be a mixture of a blood clot and a cyst. This news eased my mind even though I knew a final lab report would come later. However, I expected a good outcome and concluded I had overreacted. I blamed myself for unnecessarily creating an anxiety attack.

Approximately a week later, I visited my gynecologist for my post-op appointment. She asked how I was. I told her about the surgeon's assessment and explained that we were awaiting the final report. She mentioned that she was aware the initial pathology report had returned results that said suspicious cells were found around the edge of the cyst. She then told me further analysis was needed. This was, indeed, new information. Honestly, it shocked me. My anxiety level skyrocketed immediately, but I said nothing.

However, the next morning I called the surgeon to see if he had received the final report. He hadn't, but he verified what my gynecologist had said. He also said he felt a "funny feeling" in his spirit, which led him to pray about my situation. Then he asked for additional testing. He was awaiting the secondary analysis and agreed to call when it was received. My feeling of panic began to grow even more. Since it was a Friday, I knew the earliest I would hear from him was Monday. The weekend was horrible. My thoughts were consumed with having cancer. I truly feared that diagnosis. *I am going to die! There is no other option!*

On Monday morning, I received a personal call from my surgeon. As soon as I heard his voice, I knew the outcome was negative. Sure enough, the pathology report had confirmed the mass as cancerous. The tissue on the perimeter was extremely unusual in its composition and was of great concern! He recommended I come to his

21

office immediately to discuss more surgery. He apologized for calling, but said he knew I was anxious. In addition, he mentioned his vacation was pending, so we needed to talk *now*.

The call from my surgeon had taken less than five minutes, but felt like an eternity. I was in total shock! I felt numb and began crying. I was scared. *I have CANCER! OMG! What do I say? What should I do? This is my life!* Then I projected my anger on my surgeon. *Of all things, he tells me I have cancer and then decides to go on vacation? How could he do this? What about me? Does he not care?*

Needless to say, I was not happy with the unfortunate turn of events. I couldn't even find consolation in the manner with which I had been given this horrible news. All I felt was overwhelming fear and the uncertainty that surrounded that moment. My life was out of control!

Once I gathered my senses, I traveled to the surgeon's office. It was the best thing I could have done. He saw me immediately and teared up when he told me how sorry he was about the news. We cried together. That is when I realized how difficult this process was for him. We had become close, like siblings. I could see he was hurting and realized he was doing the best he could. Once I realized this, it made the whole situation easier to understand and accept. Still, what I really wanted to hear was a horrible mistake had been made and I didn't have cancer!!! But that was not the direction this whole story was headed!

Without a doubt, the following week was the worst in my life. My feelings were totally out of control. One minute I was laughing. The next, I was crying. I was obsessed with the thought of dying and was utterly terrified. I couldn't imagine what death would be like and was frightened about the prospect of suffering pain, especially if my illness was a protracted one. All decisions were completely overwhelming! Even the simple ones—like what to eat or what to wear— were more than I could handle. Serious decisions loomed over my head. How could I make monumental decisions when I couldn't even decide what I wanted to do the next minute?

Do I want surgery? Should it be a modified radical mastectomy or a larger lumpectomy? Should I do anything? Has the cancer spread to my lymph nodes? How much time do I have to live? Is this it? If so, how do I wish to spend my last days?
I was told there was no time to waste and I was pressured to make decisions, literally

within hours, or in one to two days, at most. It felt like I was on a roller coaster that was completely out of control. I was told the longer I waited, the more my outcome was compromised. On the other hand, time crawled by. I agonized over decisions. I talked with family and close friends. And I cried until there were no more tears. There were times I was sure I had lost my mind. I was overly preoccupied and could think of nothing else. I felt sorry for myself. I felt like anything I did was meaningless because it seemed like I had already died. *What is the point? Just let me die and get it over with!* At the same time, my life was on a "fast-forward" track. I was dealing with all the decisions I had to make and trying to handle my full range of emotions while still continuing to do my regular job in a competent manner. It was as close to an insane existence as I have ever come!

The next meeting with the surgeon confirmed my worst fears. It was not only breast cancer, but an unusual form. I had Squamous Cell Cancer (SCC), which was generally found in the lining tissues of the body. Since the breast forms out of these tissues, it was possible for this kind of cancer to occur in the breast, but it was rare!

The more common kind of breast cancer is the "in ductu" variety, or that which forms in the milk ducts. In his research, my surgeon found the only treatment recommended for my type of cancer was surgery—a modified radical mastectomy. I was familiar with it because I am a nurse, but I still questioned him. We were talking very intelligibly when a tidal wave of emotion hit me and I began to cry. All talking ceased while I sobbed uncontrollably. A nurse friend who had accompanied me stood on one side, trying to comfort me. On the other side was my surgeon with his arm around me. Then an amazing thing happened. He graciously offered his personal cell phone number and said to call any time. He didn't want me to be so troubled that I could not rest or function.

Several days later, I asked my friend if I had heard him correctly. She confirmed it. That is when I realized what an astonishing gift I was given. Of all the surgeons I have known in my nursing career, I never knew one as caring as him. The offer to call was not used, but I never forgot his kindness and empathy. He was a light when all I saw was darkness.

I felt like I had been hit by a Mack truck. In a matter of days, my whole world had come tumbling down and I was absolutely sure I would be dead in a few months!

Then I realized that odd feeling of starting on some kind of journey had actually come true!

My journey had begun that very day!

My Spiritual Lesson:

When I left the surgeon's office, I had an epiphany. My surgeon had been specifically chosen for me! God brought us together and was already at work on my behalf for my upcoming surgical event. The fact that my surgeon was a praying man and had taken time to ask for God's direction with the surgery and lab analysis made a huge difference. Without that happening, I believed my cancer might have gone undetected. For that, I was most grateful and said a prayer of thanks. At the same time, I concluded my "gut feeling" was, indeed, the Holy Spirit at work. *I think He is urging me to listen. What is He trying to tell me?* Then I reminded myself when God works, He works in magnificent ways, but the ride is often unpredictable!

Many months later, it became apparent the car door event was also a blessing in disguise. It was God's way of opening my eyes to a problem that existed—one of which I was unaware. Without the "accident" happening, the lump might not have been discovered for another year or more! I had a mammogram the month before the car incident and nothing was found. In another year, who knows what would have happened? God knew my cancer needed to be revealed! My mother asked if my "Grand Am slam" could have caused it. I knew it was not likely, but an injury could encourage cancer cells to begin their erratic growing pattern if they were present. There was no question that God intervened and saved my life!

RITA CARBUHN

THE 2nd SIGN: A WALKING PIN CUSHION

"Because He loves me," says the Lord, "I will rescue him; I will protect him, for he acknowledges my name. He will call upon me, and I will answer him; I will be with him in trouble, I will deliver him and honor him. With long life will I satisfy him and show him my salvation." (Psalms 91:14-16, NIV)

A week later, on Monday, I received a call from my former Michigan pastor. We had been friends for many years and when I moved to Kentucky, she vowed to continue being a support even though we were miles apart. She was aware of my cancer diagnosis; I had discussed my options with her. She knew I was facing impending surgery on Thursday of that week.

Although she asked about my welfare, my spirit told me there was another reason for her call.

Finally, she mentioned I had a guardian angel who would be watching over my surgery. I knew immediately she was talking about a mutual friend of ours who had been failing in her health. I asked if Frieda had died and she confirmed her passing earlier that day. I was instantly filled with a sense of emptiness. I knew she had been ill and my intention had been to call her, but I never followed through. Now it was too late!

When I got off the phone, I wept for my friend, Frieda. She was such a vibrant person with a wonderful zest for living. I admired her immensely and learned so much from her. Despite the many trials in her life, she had always found strength in her faith. We shared many stories and laughed heartily in the years we knew one another. She loved Jesus! I looked to her as an example of how I wanted to be "when I grew up" in my faith. I hoped I would be able to accept the events in my life and still feel as strongly and positively about the Lord as she did. Every time I was with her, I always learned something new about her faith and felt inspired to do better. She was a true Christian in every sense and taught me very powerful lessons about Jesus through her daily actions. Many of us looked to Frieda as a mother figure and we loved her enormously. She was one of the few persons with whom you could talk about the subject of death. We often shared our expectations of what might happen when we died. I remember discussing her impression of heaven because she had been given a glimpse of it through a near-death experience. She talked about how she was climbing steps to the Golden Gate but was pulled back before she arrived at the entrance. Despite not reaching it, she had a quick view. I remember her saying, "Rita, it was so beautiful! We just can't imagine!" She had no fear of dying and actually looked forward to her time.

I fondly recalled the first time I met Frieda. I had joined a group of women who met monthly to work on various arts and crafts projects. We each had our own special interest, but our purpose in coming together was primarily for fellowship. Since all of us belonged to the same church and worshipped together weekly, we knew one another very well. However, in the course of our gatherings, we soon discovered there was always something new to learn. We had a great time talking, sharing stories, crying, laughing, and eating. Oh, yes, the food was of prime importance. In fact, sometimes talking and eating were all we actually accomplished in an evening! We adopted our name, "The Chatterstitch Group," because we chattered on endlessly about everything while each of us was involved in some kind of a stitchery craft such as quilting, cross stitch, etc. We were famous within our church for our zany antics and our ability to laugh and have fun in everything we did. Members came and went, but our core group of ten continued meeting monthly for approximately ten years. It was during one of these gatherings when I learned Frieda had undergone a mastectomy. One evening, as she was sewing on a project, she took the pin out of her project and jammed it into her breast. She didn't react, but was well aware I was watching. I cringed at the thought of how much it must have hurt. Frieda noticed the shock on my face and began laughing. She then revealed she had a foam prosthesis and had discovered it worked well as her pin cushion! We laughed over this event and it very quickly became the unofficial initiation for all new members. Frieda would wait for an opportune moment to stick a pin in her fake boob and watch the reaction of the new member. She loved the shock value and I know she had fun with it. In fact, we all did. Frieda was a great example of how to live after having a mastectomy. When I first met her, I never gave a mastectomy a second thought. Now, with my own cancer diagnosis, it assumed a different reality.

With her death, I knew Frieda was in a better place. She was reunited with her husband, other family members, and special friends. I felt happy for her, but sad for us who remained behind. We all loved her deeply and missed her terribly. Of course, I felt extremely guilty for having not called her in the last months of her life. I think it is only right to say goodbye to a good friend when their time on Earth may be limited, but what had I done? Absolutely nothing!!! I had allowed myself to get busy and not make one simple phone call. At that moment, I made a vow not to become so preoccupied with my life that I would overlook the importance of contacting a friend. There are so many actions and kindnesses we can offer daily to show God's love but talking to one another was the simplest. It was likely the most meaningful action I could have taken, but I missed my opportunity. I had failed miserably as a friend!

Remembering Frieda helped to get in touch with my own feelings about death and dying. I always believed I was unafraid because of my strong Christian faith and my belief in the hereafter. If I faced death, I expected to be able to accept it easily. However, it was very simple to rationalize my feelings when I wasn't looking death squarely in the eye. Now that I was suddenly faced with the very real prospect, it became a totally different matter. The diagnosis of cancer forced me to deal with the issue of dying head-on. I was aware many people view cancer as an automatic death sentence and it is easy to "give up." I didn't want to be someone who took that approach. I knew modern treatment methods had changed the outcome drastically and cancer was no longer synonymous with dying. Then again, I was no longer sure what my reality was. My world had been turned upside down. I was confused. I couldn't take life for granted any more. I had too much living yet to do. I believed God had more of life waiting for me and I had a purpose to fulfill. Besides, I was too young to die! I was only 47!

One of the processes that is normal to experience when you face death is to review your life and determine its value. Frieda's passing propelled me into this process. I thought of the things I hadn't done, the places I hadn't been, and the people I would not see again. I grieved for my mother and brother, who would be the lone survivors of our immediate family; for my nephew, whom I would never see grow to adulthood; and for my dogs, who were too old to adjust to living with someone else. *Who will take care of them?* I thought about the people I had known throughout my life. *What they will say about me?* I once told my Michigan pastor I wanted a memorial service while still alive so I would know what others would say. At the time, we both laughed, but I was serious. It seemed so sad that we would wait until someone died to express our love and admiration.

I reflected on my past love relationships and thought about three men in particular. One man, who became my fiancé, I met while living in California. Our impending marriage was the reason I moved to Michigan. Even though the wedding arrangements had been finalized, he backed out one week before the actual day. Within a matter of minutes, our relationship ended abruptly over the phone! I was devastated. When I learned he married his high school sweetheart within two months, it was a double whammy. I was extremely hurt and depressed over the failure and lost all faith in men. For four years, I chose not to date because I allowed that experience to have a negative influence over subsequent relationships. I also recalled my feelings of shame and distrust and remembered how painful they were. Finally, I obtained professional help to resolve my issues, which resulted in me becoming a much happier person. Then, twenty years later, I saw him again and had the opportunity to share in person the emotional pain he inflicted on me. I felt cleansed after our conversation and thanked God for allowing that heavy burden to be lifted from my heart.

I thought about another man. I was involved with him for over ten years. We never married but, in my heart, I always felt like we were. Our relationship had been put to many tests and we survived most of them by becoming closer. I knew he would always have a special place in my heart because I so completely loved him. At the same time, I had lost sight of my own identity. This issue became the final test in our relationship and it was the one we didn't overcome. Once again, with professional help, I realized I needed to leave this relationship to rediscover myself. Even so, I still cared deeply for him and leaving was the most difficult decision I have ever made regarding a relationship. Fortunately, the two of us maintained a friendship over the years, which alleviated some of my pain.

With the third man, I wondered if I had done the right thing in deciding to change our relationship. Even though we dated for several months, I decided to see someone else exclusively. He accepted my decision to be friends—our paths crossed frequently because of similar professional interests, so we were able to maintain our friendship easily.

Over the years, as I moved in and out of my relationships, I often thought about him and how much I still cared. I never took the risk of telling him, however. It seemed like one or the other of us was committed elsewhere and our timing was out of sync. We both accepted this fact and lived our separate lives. However, we always kept in contact. I thanked God for him, but also wondered what might have happened if we connected.

Finally, I reflected about how I always wanted a lifelong, loving husband and marriage, but it was the one thing I was never able to achieve. Then I cried for the children and the grandchildren I never had. I wondered what my family would do with my possessions, many of which had wonderful memories attached to them. I realized my family didn't know the stories about the articles. In cleaning the house after my death, this would escape their knowledge and they would only be struck with the amount of work they faced sorting through them.

I thought about my father, who died in 1985. I knew I would see him in heaven. Over the years, I have missed him and wondered what he would think of the person I had become. I tried to guess his impression of my current struggle. Although I would love seeing him again, I wasn't ready to join him. I wondered what people at work would say and if they would even miss me because I was so new at the job. I thought about my friends in Michigan and others who lived all over the U.S. *Will they care? Will they miss me? Will they even remember me? Why did God bring me to Kentucky? Was it to die here? Why would God do such a thing?*

And then I felt intense anger with God! *It isn't right, God! It's not fair!*

If I had the chance to live my life over again, would I change anything?

My answer was an unequivocal NO. I regretted nothing. Yet, being totally honest with myself, I knew there were a few different turns in the road I would like to have tried. I wondered what changes would have occurred, had I taken one of those paths. Despite those brief musings, I felt my life had been a success. I had chosen a career I thoroughly enjoyed and had worked happily for over 26 years. I had all the material possessions I needed and was never without anything I ever wanted. I had taken care of myself quite well, had traveled extensively, and had many wonderful friends located throughout the country. I truly felt happy and content with what I had achieved and for the person I had become.

I thought about designing my memorial service and writing my obituary. I considered making a video so I could share my thoughts. I wanted to tell my family and friends how important they were. It was their love, support, and friendships that gave my life meaning and made it wonderful. They brought joy as well as sorrow, but loving them was what life was all about. I pondered a phrase which formed my basic philosophy for life. It was the tenet, "Life is love and to love is to live." Yes, loving was what life was all about, but now I faced losing everything because of my cancer.

Once I grieved my losses, I turned my attention to living. I was suddenly overcome by a sense of exquisite and unexplainable peace, as if all my anxieties had completely disappeared. In that brief moment, I felt God was reassuring me that I would live. Strange as it may sound, I also believed if He wanted me to die, He wouldn't have permitted Frieda to pass. It made no sense, but it was how I felt. It comforted me to know she would be present spiritually during my surgery. With her as my guardian angel, I believed God was giving me a special blessing as well as another positive sign. What He required of me was to trust Him completely.

My Spiritual Lesson:

Taking the time to review my history and recalling the events associated with my life was a much-needed task. In fact, I thought about the value of doing it on a more regular basis rather than waiting until I was facing a life crisis! Remembering my past allowed me to take stock of my life. It was my story and had gotten me to where I was today. It was unique to me and only God knew every detail intimately. In fact, He probably knew the details even better than me because His knowledge is so vast. After all, He created me and has known what is truly in my heart since before I came into being. I, on the other hand, have judged my life from my own humanness, which has very limited parameters.

Yes, God had accompanied me on this journey of life whether I was aware of His presence or not. He has always been by my side. It made little sense to determine whether I would change my past, because that was simply not possible. Instead, the real question was whether I could love the person I had become. *Can I love me as Jesus loves me? Can I forgive myself for what I'm not? Am I thankful for the life God has given me? Am I, indeed, what God created me to be?*

To show my gratitude to Him, I wrote Him a letter.

Father God,

Thank you for loving me just as I am. You knew me before I was formed in my mother's womb and I have been fearfully and wonderfully made in Your image. You have loved me every day of my life and have promised to love me for eternity. There is nothing better than a relationship with You. I am proud to be your child and I look forward to being Your bride. I love You!

Your daughter,
Rita.

At that point, I had still not answered my own questions about whether or not I could love myself as Jesus loves me, forgive myself, and love the person I became. As time passed, however, I found these answers.

RITA CARBUHN

THE 3rd SIGN: GOD'S TEARS AND SMILES

"Wait for the Lord; be strong and take heart and wait for the Lord." (Psalms 27:14, NIV)

For over ten years, I was involved in a weekly Christian share group. As a nurse having worked in behavioral health, I was comfortable with groups, but I had never been in a faith-oriented group until my Michigan pastor started one. I was a charter member and benefitted from it enormously. I considered it a gift from Jesus because it was so special. With the very unique combination of the share group, the church to which I belonged, and the loving guidance of my pastor, I grew tremendously in my faith. For the first time in my life, I developed a personal relationship with Jesus and came to know and love Him in a more intimate way.

In earlier years, my life had church in it, but I was involved more in the activities than in worship. I knew stories about Jesus, but I didn't know Him. I didn't understand the impact Jesus could have on my life if we developed a relationship. In fact, I'm not even sure I understood what having a relationship with Jesus meant. My previous ministers had never spoken about this aspect of faith, so it was a concept foreign to me. I prayed and read the Bible while in church, or if I was preparing for a class, but it was rare to do this at other times. Even though I attended church and Sunday school as a young child, I was never baptized. My parents did not agree with infant baptism. They believed I should make that choice when I was older and able to understand its meaning. I chose baptism while in high school and think my close relationship with my pastor was why I did it. Yet, I don't think I truly understood its full meaning back then. During high school, I was involved in many youth activities in the church as well as the choir. Even so, I was not fully committed because my studying and other interests took priority over church. This pattern of avoidance continued through my college and graduate school years when religious involvement of any kind was eliminated. Simply put, Jesus was not a part of my life because I had moved away from Him.

The point at which I had the closest relationship with the Lord was when I lived in California. At that time, I belonged to a Presbyterian Church. That particular church was unconventional. Almost everything about that church was different. First of all, the congregation was primarily Black and I was one of the small White minority. This opened my eyes toward another culture and helped to see life from their perspective. The church had both traditional and contemporary services in which I was involved. However, I preferred the latter because it included singing and playing guitars in a more upbeat style. This type of worship music was new and rare in churches. I had never found a church that incorporated anything other than organ music, but I had heard California was doing something different. I was eager to locate a church that included this new worship style.

Once I got settled in San Diego, I found one. Honestly, what appealed to me was the music. Having played clarinet for over fifteen years, music was a significant part of my life. I enjoyed all genres of music from classical, rock, and jazz to gospel. For me, it was an integral part of my worship experience. I also loved being in the choir as it provided a special kind of joy in worshipping my Lord. I enjoyed singing the old hymns and knew them well. Many members in the new church were involved in writing music for our contemporary service.

Our choir often sang at Christian concerts throughout southern California. We made records and were featured on several radio and TV stations. It was all new and very thrilling. An exciting part of our worship services were the ecumenical services we shared with two other churches. One was a

Hispanic Catholic Church and the other was Lutheran. Neither was traditional, so they meshed easily with us. The ecumenical services happened on a monthly rotation and the presence of the Holy Spirit was palpable. I loved every aspect of our contemporary environment. It expanded my views on worship and helped me share my love of the Lord with other believers.

Our church expanded into other arenas as well. We were extremely involved in the social issues of the day and had a ministry to help others who were less fortunate. We picked up homeless people in downtown San Diego and brought them to our church on Sunday afternoons for a free meal. There was no sermon delivered, which caused a lot of suspicion because they would often ask, "When does the minister talk?" Word got out to the homeless and our group expanded each week. It was such a blessing to be involved in this ministry. We also supported other social issues. For example, we worked with the migrant workers and supported the grape boycotts. The church had a loosely-formed Biblical structure that was typical of the California environment in the early seventies.

I taught junior and senior high Sunday school classes. One of the projects we did was to make a movie about God's love as evidenced by the actions of everyday people. Not only did the students film people's lives, but they supported their examples with scripture. It was a very creative effort and was well received by the church members. It was clearly a "California" thing to do! I liked the way our church functioned and my faith grew enormously. Most of all, I recognized I was a child of God who belonged to the Lord. It was that feeling of "belonging" I liked immensely!

When I moved to Michigan, I could not find a church that met my needs. I had been spoiled in California. Unfortunately, it was a different environment and this new type of worship service didn't exist there. For a while, I participated in private services with four contemporary, Sisters of Mercy nuns. I played guitar and we sang and prayed together. It was delightfully different. However, after six months, our group disbanded. The nuns were moved to other assignments and, suddenly, they were gone. I was left behind and began my search again.

After months of not finding anything, I felt discouraged and concluded I no longer needed a church. I recognized there was a void in my life, but I didn't consider it could be the lack of a relationship with God or because my spiritual journey had gone awry.

Little did I realize how that void would become a chasm.

As the years passed, I found myself searching for things to fill the hole, but nothing worked. This separation continued for ten years, at which point I met a woman who changed the direction of my life. We met at work and seemed to hit it off immediately. She actually felt like a long-lost sister. She attended a small Methodist church and kept inviting me to join her. I wasn't interested because I didn't think I needed church. I thought it was unnecessary. Honestly, I was scared to return because I had been away for so long. I knew my relationship with God was distant because I had created my own alienation. I was certain He wouldn't be interested in me.

God is so wise and wonderful. He knew my fears and understood exactly what I needed. When my friend's invitations fell on deaf ears, God urged her to ask me to speak to her Sunday school class. She wanted her youth to be educated on drugs and alcohol, which was right up my alley as a mental health nurse. I accepted the invitation and decided to stay for the church service following the class. I didn't realize how much God was preparing the way for my return. He simply reached into my heart and plucked a few of my heartstrings! I was personally touched by Him and didn't even know it. I had such fun teaching the class, but when I listened to the choir singing in the service afterwards, I realized how much I missed singing. I introduced myself to the director and immediately joined the choir that day. This meant driving seventeen miles one way to practice on Wednesday evenings and then repeating this plan on Sundays for church services. It felt so good being back in church again!

Gradually, I came to realize the void in my life was both a lack of a relationship with God and a lack of corporate worship. I found my needs being met in the church. I also felt a sense of belonging with the other members and, more importantly, with God. In March 1986, I accepted Jesus as my Lord and Savior and was born again.

As time passed, the church services, the committee meetings, and the many volunteer responsibilities became an ever-increasing part of my life. One thing led to another and, before long, my entire life revolved around the church and its members. My closest friends were other members. I felt very content. My void had finally been filled! There was a downside, however. A relationship of ten plus years came to an end. Although I was saddened by the loss, it was something that felt right.

My friends at church supported me during this difficult time and I knew it was time to move. I sold my house and purchased a new one in the small town where the church was located. This move lengthened the drive to work by some twenty miles one way, but I didn't mind. I felt settled and, for the first time, I could see myself remaining in the community for the rest of my life.

Unbeknownst to us, sometimes God has another plan that is set in action and becomes clear later. This was my story. The contentment in my life didn't last long. Within two years, there were severe disruptions at work which resulted in major job changes. Numerous reorganizations, changes in administrative staff, and layoffs became commonplace. The stress was constant and overwhelming! I found myself distressed, upset, and irritable on a daily basis. Both my work and life had lost their joy.

After realizing I couldn't continue to live in that manner and knowing I couldn't accept some of the changes occurring at work, I decided it was time to leave my employment. Having worked there for close to 22 years, I was faced with a difficult, but necessary, decision. I disagreed with many of the philosophies that were being supported and knew I could no longer be effective in my role. Besides, one of my former coworkers had become my boss. Honestly, that was the final straw. I updated my resume and began my search. I expected it would take a year before I could locate an appropriate position.

However, jobs began presenting themselves immediately. Amazingly, within six months, I had interviewed for and accepted a job in Kentucky. The period from December, when I submitted my resignation, to February, when I actually moved, was a blur of activity. I said goodbye to my church family and a very extensive support system, left a job I had loved for much of my life, and resigned from my numerous professional activities! In three short months, my life was dramatically altered. What was so amazing is the fact that I believed the move was being orchestrated by God and that this job change was part of His plan. I felt obedience was what He asked of me and so I took the big step!

When I arrived in Kentucky, I immediately set about the business of finding a new church. Since I had accepted the fact that church membership was now an essential part of my life, I was certain I would not function well until I found a new church home. However, after months of visiting churches and being the new and unknown person everywhere I went, I lost patience with the process. Although there were nine United Methodist churches in town, I only visited five. I soon learned being a single person and attending a new church was an extremely lonely task.

In many of the churches, the only person who acknowledged me was the pastor. This was definitely not the way I thought it should be! Most people smiled, but said nothing. In one large church I attended two Sundays in a row, not even one person talked to me! I was totally flabbergasted! Since I came from a very warm and loving church where members freely gave one another hugs and were genuinely concerned when someone missed a service, I felt unloved and unwanted, almost like a stranger in a foreign land. I desperately missed the hugs from my "family."

That all changed on Ash Wednesday when I found a small, country church that felt like home. I was greeted at the door with a hug and immediately accepted as one of their own. It was truly wonderful! That feeling of belonging never dissipated and I joined the church within the month.

Despite the fact that I had found a new church and had a job where I was making new friends, I was desperately lonely. I missed my Michigan friends and church family, but soon learned that "out of sight" meant I was also out of people's minds. My name was removed from the next printing of the Michigan church address book even though they assured me I would always be considered part of their membership. Numerous people vowed to keep in touch, but I heard nothing. Even when I wrote them, there was no response. Within a couple of months, I felt forgotten, abandoned, and actually dismissed by my former church family. I was hurt and angry. I couldn't believe what was happening or how I was being treated.

I even talked to my new pastor one Sunday about my feelings and he suggested we pray together. It was then I realized I needed more prayer in my life. My pastor told me he got up every day at 0400 and prayed for two hours to start his day. I was astounded to hear this, but I took his example as a needed lesson.

It was time to develop a more personal relationship with Jesus, which I could accomplish through prayer. I needed to rely more on God's leading in my life rather than trying to do everything on my own. Instead of focusing on my hurt feelings, I asked the Lord to show me what He wanted me to do in Kentucky. That very day, it became apparent He wanted me to open my eyes to what was happening around me and accept what He was providing.

Because I was missing the fellowship and support of a share group, it made sense to find another one. I thought it would help me make new friends and give me the support I was missing. It would also provide the opportunity to deal with my faith issues I had put on hold while I made the move. I talked to a coworker who was a member of a share group and asked if she knew of a group that was looking for new members. She didn't, but promised to keep me in mind. Within a couple of months, her group began accepting new members and she told me about the opportunity. I jumped at the chance. From the very first meeting, I knew God had led me to a group of women who were sincere with their spiritual pilgrimages. I felt the Holy Spirit's presence and believed they would challenge me to grow in my faith. God has an interesting way of making things happen! When I am honest with myself, I have to acknowledge Jesus knows my needs best. But it also seems I need to be reminded frequently! I apparently don't learn this lesson well! I always think I know better than Him and have a long history of trying to control my life rather than resting in His guidance. I fight against God and make it difficult for Him to use me in purposeful ways. On the other hand, I know if He really wants me to do something in particular, He will tell me, somehow. For example, shortly after I joined the Michigan church, I became aware that Jesus was urging me to turn the control of my life over to Him. Gradually, I learned this lesson. In fact, the primary reason I took the risk of moving was because I felt He was leading me there. For the first time in my life, I placed the entire job situation in His hands and prayed for His will to be done. I told Him I was ready to do whatever He wanted me to do. Amazingly, all paths led to Kentucky! Everything fit so smoothly in such an intricate pattern that I knew it had to be God who orchestrated it all. I didn't understand why, but knew in my heart it was where I needed to be. I was sure to learn God's reason, in His time. Meanwhile, my tasks were to be patient and wait. Be still and know He is God!

My Spiritual Lesson:

The share group turned out to be the perfect gift from God. I was led to the group only two weeks before I was diagnosed with cancer! At a point when I felt totally abandoned (from God as well as my Michigan church and friends), He gave me the chance to belong again. He shared His love through the group members. I obviously needed support in a much different way than how I first envisioned it. God knew what I needed and created the opportunity for me to join the group. He was aware I was about to embark on a difficult journey in which I would need additional strength, love, and support. He also knew that each of the group members would share their innermost thoughts and feelings and, through this process, our tears and smiles would also be His. The group was God's gift to carry me through the darkness that was about to descend!

I cannot overlook the fact that tears are very precious to God. In fact, we are promised in scripture that He collects each one in a bottle that is labeled specifically with our name and recorded in His book (Psalm 56:8, New Living Translation). It is a beautiful image of God and demonstrates the power and depth of His love. No tear is wasted. If He collects each one, then He treasures ALL of them. He will honor each tear in some way. Although I don't know how or when that will happen, I trust this is another of His promises. I know there will be a day in eternity where He will wipe away every tear that is shed, so I have to believe, from God's perspective, my tears become His keepsakes. How awesome is this?

THE 4th SIGN: CHIRPS OF LIFE

"But those who hope in the Lord will renew their strength. They shall soar on wings like eagles; they will run and not grow weary, they will walk and not be faint." (Isaiah 40:31, NIV)

Before I entered the hospital for surgery, I noticed a small brown bird frequenting a hanging plant on my front porch. She piqued my curiosity when I realized she was building a nest! However, despite my initial excitement, I found it odd that she had chosen my beautiful ivy geranium as her new home. Throughout the neighborhood, there were many trees—every kind imaginable!—that would have made a good home for her nest. Why did she have to choose my plant in which to lay her eggs? I felt annoyed because of the mess she was making on my porch and the fact that it hampered the beauty of my plant. Daily, I found the remnants of her nest-building strewn everywhere, which irritated me. I soon learned that, whenever I would try to sweep the porch or water my plant, I would frighten her.

As the days passed, this began to concern me. I didn't want to take the chance of permanently sending her away and cause her to abandon the nest. Suddenly I felt a check in my spirit. *Perhaps I need to view this event differently! Could this be part of God's plan? What does it mean?* I knew God doesn't work by happenstance, so there had to be a purpose greater than the obvious.

That is when the nesting experience took on the symbolism of my life and death. I couldn't explain why, but I believed my future depended on these birds hatching. It then became even more important for Momma bird not to abandon her babies! At that moment, my irritation was transformed into feelings of wonder and awe because I was being given a rare opportunity to share in a "birth" experience. Once I comprehended how magnificent this gift was, I decided to participate fully in all the events—from the safety of my dining room window, where I would not disturb them!

Day after day, I watched Momma bird. She was busy with her task. She flew about the neighborhood gathering treasures and quickly fashioned a strong but ordinary-looking nest. Then she laid her five eggs. I counted them one day when she was gone. Then her true work began. Patience became her greatest ally as she sat on the eggs, hour after hour, day after day, waiting for them to hatch. I knew this time was a very critical period so I became even more cautious with my movements on the porch. Before I ventured out to do anything (like getting the mail), I waited until Momma bird was actually gone. When she flew off to get her food, I quickly emerged from the house to do my tasks. I was very sensitive to her coming and going because I wanted to make sure her eggs would hatch.

On the day I left for the hospital, there was still no change. Momma bird continued to sit on the eggs and wait. I asked my friend, Trisha, who was staying at the house, to watch over the bird and her nest. I shared my fears and concerns with her, and asked her to be careful with her movements, too. She agreed and timed her front porch duties to be in sync with Momma bird's actions.

The day before my hospital discharge, Trisha reported the eggs had hatched. She heard the chirping. Once I got home, I was anxious to check on them because I felt they were as much mine as Momma bird's! I also felt an even greater burden to be careful and not do anything that would scare her. I listened to the chirps of new life. They were wondrous sounds! It was almost as if they were singing praises to our Lord! Of course, I waited for Momma bird to fly away so I could sneak a peek. When she did, I ran outside to pull the planter from its hook. What I saw was a beautiful sight! Five soft little bodies were snuggled together in the nest. I marveled at how young they were and how they could all fit into the nest. Since they were asleep, I quickly replaced the plant and left.

Shortly after my exit, Momma bird returned. This immediately set off a raucous round of chirps and squeals. As I watched from a window, she patiently fed each baby. Soon, the chirping stopped. Everyone was satisfied and went to sleep. This ritual was repeated often while the babies grew in size. Pretty soon, their little heads were peeking over the top of the planter.

As I watered my plant one morning after Momma had vacated it, I was greeted with five eager, open beaks. Of course, I didn't have food. I was very carefully watering my plant so I could keep it alive and was focused on how to do this without drowning the chicks. I also didn't want to ruin their nest. I replaced the plant on its hook, and when I turned to leave, I noticed Momma bird sitting on a nearby fence, watching me.

I quickly made my exit, but wondered if I had made a mistake by looking in the plant. I meant no harm to her babies and hoped she understood my intentions. Her calm demeanor crept into my heart and filled me with an overwhelming sense of admiration and appreciation for God's creatures.

In the days that followed, I took more risks. I actually wandered out on the porch to sit in a chair so I could watch and wait. Even so, I still remained at a distance from the nest— out of respect. Momma seemed comfortable with my presence and continued her daily tasks. Since I was aware the babies had grown, I was hoping to see them take flight. I had never been privy to such an event before and it was something I wanted to witness. Unfortunately, it was not a privilege I was offered.

One day, I came home to absolute silence. I knew what it meant—the nest was empty! When I checked, I was right. The birds were gone! They never returned. Interestingly, my feelings were an odd mixture of happiness and sorrow. I was glad all five birds had a new life but, at the same time, I was saddened they would no longer be part of mine!

We become aware of God's presence in our own unique ways. If we truly allow ourselves to "see" the events that unfold around us and to acknowledge the unique patterns our lives follow, I don't think we can draw a conclusion other than to realize God is very much a part of everything. We should be able to see God's guidance, direction, and actions in our lives. For me, this was the case with the birds. They came to represent my life and my relationship with God. I felt the birds were a sign of assurance that He was available to nurture me both spiritually and physically, just as Momma cared for her young. The odd thing was the connection I made in my mind that, if the eggs did not hatch and the birds did not mature to adulthood, it meant I would not live. There was no logic to this belief, but I was convinced it was true. The mere fact of the nest being prepared and the eggs being laid prior to my hospitalization were symbolic of the fact I was beginning the process of rebirth, too. I was about to "hatch" my own eggs, but mine were spiritual in nature!

From these events, perhaps I was to learn the difficult lesson of patience, which Momma knew only too well. And just like Momma nurtured her babies, God was nurturing me. I was reminded He is only a heartbeat away. He is our very breath of life! He is willing to give all the nourishment we need and it will satisfy us so completely that we will want no more. We only have to ask and make our needs known through prayer (our "chirpings") and He is by our side instantly. Usually, it is us who have left Him in the first place. Momma bird knew her role innately. It is too bad we don't always know the role we should take in our relationship with Christ. I honestly think we lack trust with Jesus. How wonderful would it be if all our actions spoke to the fact that "for in Him we live and move and have our being"? (Acts 17:28, NIV)

The day Momma watched me quietly from the fence reminded me of the way God watches over each of us. We know He is there, for He said, "I am with you always" (Matthew 28:20, NIV). For some reason, we often seem to question His presence and intentions. Yet, our Christian faith tells us God remains available on the sidelines, ready and waiting. He doesn't try to interfere in our lives until we ask for His guidance. Perhaps the most difficult lesson to accept is the fact He doesn't judge or criticize us.

As humans, we cannot make sense of a love so complete and so unjustified. Surely, this can't be! But we are told repeatedly He merely loves us as we are, while He watches and waits for us to come to Him. How we must break His heart with our human ways! Nonetheless, He allows us to use our free will to go our own way even though the path we choose is not the one He would have us travel. I believe sometimes He waits for us to establish the conditions (good and bad) that allow Him to enter our lives.

When we finally recognize our need and desire for Him, and make this need known, He immediately begins working actively to help us accomplish His goals.

Our prayers are much like the chirpings of birds! When we are so desperately in need of something or find ourselves in situations out of our control, that is the time we think about praying and start our incessant "chirping." We often don't associate our daily lives, tasks, and functioning with our prayer life until there is a crisis of some sort! Then our prayers take on a frantic quality and we want instant relief. If the answer comes quickly, we conclude, "Yes! Oh, that was good and easy!" and we turn our attention to the next thing. For all intents and purposes, we forget about God until the next crisis. We may even fool ourselves into thinking we were responsible and God had no part in it. When there is no perceived answer to our prayers, we feel frustrated or angry and decide praying doesn't really work. It doesn't produce what we thought it promised! But how wrong we are if this becomes our pattern!

The Lord is my witness that I have taken both approaches in my life. However, through my experience with cancer, I learned God wants us to pray for all things. He did tell us to "pray continually" (I Thessalonians 5:17, NIV). He truly wants to participate in each moment, but He does require us to speak up and ask for what we need. I heard Naomi Judd, the country singer, say, "Pray for the answer, not for the problem." I think this is good advice.

The Bible assures us our prayers will be answered. "Ask, and it will be given to you; seek, and you will find; knock and it will be opened to you. For everyone who asks receives, and he who seeks finds, and to him who knocks it will be opened" (Matthew 7:7-8, Revised Standard Version). This scripture is a beautiful promise. He doesn't use the word "may"; the reassuring word is "WILL"! Believing we will be given an answer to our prayers takes a tremendous amount of faith and is not easy to do. One should not take this task lightly!

Someone once told me God "cleanses" our prayers, which means He filters out what is unnecessary and answers them in ways which make sense for our unique, individual needs. I like this analogy. It verifies He truly is in control of what happens and is always busy fashioning and creating the best answer. This is truly exciting!

I have believed for some time that God knows my every need, but it has taken much longer to understand what this means. Knowing our needs isn't the same as acting on His infinite wisdom. I always thought it was unnecessary to tell Him what I need, especially because He has a better understanding of my needs. Then, one day, it suddenly occurred why it is important to ask. My asking involves commitment and participation. Our relationship would have little meaning if I did nothing and just expected Him to provide.

By asking for what I need, I have moved from a passive role to an active one. This action reveals to God that I want the two of us to maintain a dynamic relationship—that is, one which will continue to change as I grow spiritually. It is a very special relationship because it is one of grace. I believe we are all expected to participate in prayer as recognition of His love and power. It is part of God's plan to have everything work together for the good of those who love Him! He depends on our praying for His will to be fulfilled!

One thing I learned well during my journey with cancer was the power of prayer. Most of the time I tried to pray without stopping, but I soon discovered this was simply not possible when I felt very weak and burdened. When my "well" ran dry, I could not even form the thoughts in my mind, let alone utter words from my lips. It was all I could do to close my eyes and plead, *DEAR GOD, PLEASE HELP ME NOW!*

I remember this happening one day while I was receiving a chemo treatment. I felt on the verge of panic and thought I couldn't stand even one more minute of the insanity.

I wanted to rip the IV lines out of my body and run out of the room screaming, but knew that would upset everyone and they would think I had lost it, so that was not an option. Out of desperation, I closed my eyes and prayed fervently. It was simply a very desperate plea for help! I called it my "Gethsemane moment" because, like Jesus, I prayed for my cup to be taken. It was my will I desired, not His. After several minutes, when I opened my eyes, the nurse mentioned she had found the answer to a question I had asked earlier. She didn't have the heart to awaken me because I was sleeping so peacefully.

I looked at her like she was crazy and exclaimed, "Sleeping? I wasn't sleeping. I was praying like I have never prayed before, just to remain in this room!"

She was surprised with my reply and said, "Well, it must be working because you certainly had a look of peace on your face!"

I thought about that comment for weeks afterward. *How could there be peace on my face when I felt only panic and turmoil in my heart?* The only answer that made sense was Jesus. It had to be Him! In his book, *The Circle Maker*, Mark Batterson described this moment perfectly: "Sometimes the power of prayer is the power to carry on. It doesn't always change your circumstances, but it gives you the strength to walk through them. When you pray through, the burden is taken off your shoulders and put on the shoulders of Him who carried the cross to Calvary."

That is what happened to me. I had many of those days. When they came, I was certain there was nothing left inside to share in my prayers with Him. I merely laid myself before Him because that was all I could do. I rested in His arms and allowed myself to be held. That is when the Holy Spirit stepped in and took over. God heard the Spirit's pleadings on my behalf and He knew what they meant. This was an act of shameless supplication and I thank God for that loving opportunity.

I wasn't the only one involved in this kind of prayer. There were several prayer vigils organized for me. Many friends as well as strangers spent their time praying on my behalf. I was definitely touched through this intercessory prayer. I also know firsthand that it works!

All I can say is, "Thank you, Father God, for hearing the prayers of many."

Mark Batterson also stated, "We pray out of our ignorance, but God answers out of omniscience. We pray out of our impotence, but God answers out of His omnipotence.

God has the ability to answer the prayers we should have prayed but lacked the knowledge or ability to even ask. The greatest moments in life are the miraculous moments when human impotence and divine omnipotence intersect."

My Spiritual Lesson:

Why did it take having cancer to open my eyes and allow me to see the Lord's presence around me? Was it because I lost sight of the important things in life? Why is it, even now, I still continue to fight the very notion that He is in my life, intimately, on a daily basis? If I accepted this fact, would it change how I live? Would it affect how I make decisions?

Of course! It means giving up my very strong ego—the sense of power which says I, alone, have the ability to do all things. It means turning over all control to Him— agreeing to follow in His steps and responding to His will, every moment of my life. It means measuring all decisions based on what He would do. It means "living by faith, not by sight" (2 Corinthians 5:7, NIV) and acknowledging He is all I need. I know He will provide sufficiently in every way, but do I really trust that? It means realizing that the same God who spoke the universe into existence is the same God who oversees my life. He has never left me and never will. I am assured His answers to my prayers will return one day. In the interim, I know my Lord is always with me. Most of all, it means loving others, including myself, even when I don't feel like loving anyone.

Yes, all of these realizations require distinct changes be made in my life, but they are ones I believe Jesus has been urging for some time. I feel He is moving me ever closer to Him, especially in the direction of totally yielding my whole life to Him. However, He knows it is my decision whether or not I will do this. Meanwhile, He WAITS!

"Surely, He took up our pain and bore our suffering, yet we considered him punished by God, stricken by Him, and afflicted. But he was pierced for our transgressions, he was crushed for our iniquities; the punishment that brought us peace was on him, and by his wounds we are healed. We all, like sheep, have gone astray, each of us has turned to our own way; and the Lord has laid on him the iniquity of us all." (Isaiah 53:4-6, NIV)

THE 5th SIGN: SIXTEEN CHANCES

"For we know that if the earthly tent we live in is destroyed, we have a building from God, an eternal house in heaven, not built by human hands." (2 Corinthians 5:1, NIV)

Prior to surgery, I was depressed and cried easily. Whenever I told others I was planning to have a mastectomy, I usually burst into tears. I never considered any other option because I felt it was my only chance for survival. I had been informed my mass was a mixture of a blood clot and a cyst with cancerous cells on the perimeter. This worried me. I wondered if the cancer had already spread (metastasized) to other parts of my body. By having surgery, I would know if there was any lymph node involvement and it would give me a clearer indication of my prognosis. Knowing this information, of course, would help me prepare for what was to come. We had already performed a lumpectomy, so I felt my options were a mastectomy or nothing. I was unable to tolerate the idea of doing nothing and waiting. Surgery seemed the only logical answer.

Funny I should talk about logic—there was nothing logical about the feelings I was experiencing in the period between my diagnosis and surgery! Those days had a surrealistic quality. I went about my daily functions in a daze. I don't remember much other than my emotions were on a rollercoaster ride that was going wild. I knew my feelings would be labile. What I didn't expect was to experience the entire gamut of them within a time space of one to three minutes, a hundred times a day! Seriously, this is no exaggeration! I would start talking about something and the next thing I knew, I was crying—AGAIN. It didn't make any difference if the topic was a happy or sad one. My tears were uncontrollable and came at the most inopportune times. I knew I would experience a wide range of emotions because that is a normal part of the grief process and, essentially, I was grieving the loss of my breast. The stages were the same as if I had lost a family member to death—shock, denial, and disbelief. I also passed through stages of anger, bargaining, and depression. The final stage of acceptance was yet to come—it was a concept only in my head because it seemed such a long way off.

I decided to have a mastectomy without a simultaneous breast reconstruction because I thought I would better accept my reality by not seeing a breast. I wanted to witness my altered body because I thought it would make the process easier. I was deluded and should have known better. Accepting changes to my body proved to be more difficult than I imagined. Intellectually, I could understand, but emotionally, it made no sense! My reality hit me square in my face! I had become a deformed and marked woman because of my cancer! I felt ugly and unlovable. I was certain I would never again be attractive to a man and would never find the husband I desired. I even wondered if I could accept my new self! Then my mind would switch and I would tell myself I was being over-reactive and ridiculous! I was sure others could and would accept the new me, but first I had to love myself. My feelings jumped from one extreme to the other, constantly, and it was very frightening. This was not my usual method of coping.

Among my closest friends, I had always been the one to joke about my breast size. I thought I was permitted to do this since I was referring to myself and was careful to never make fun of anyone else. Despite my small size, I was very comfortable with what God had given me. I told my girlfriends all I needed was a training bra, but they didn't make them for a 40-year old woman. We laughed and they would say, "Oh, Rita, you are just exaggerating!" I knew I wasn't. I could easily have gone without a bra and no one would have known it. In fact, purchasing a bra was one of the most exasperating experiences of my life that I had to endure. I told the clerks I was hard to fit and their reply was I had not found someone trained well enough to assist me. When the fitting began, we both would get frustrated because nothing worked. I actually had one clerk say, "You are right. You have nothing!" Okay, I was right, but I surely didn't want to hear her claim it! I felt worse. I tried to reason with myself—if I was accustomed to not having large breasts anyway, why was I so upset at having one removed? It wasn't as if I was losing a major part of my identity! *Rita, how stupid is that? It's your identity as a woman that is being lost!* Breasts were part of my womanhood and their size had nothing to do with it. As a psychiatric nurse, I should have come to that conclusion. However, sometimes, when dealing with a personal issue, as this one was, one's thinking can become clouded. Such was the case for me.

Society and the media teach us women to establish our identities on the basis of our physical features. We believe we aren't worthy or lovable unless we have a thin, shapely body with large, beautiful breasts; rounded, firm buttocks; long, lean legs; and a head full of long, thick hair. I don't know many women who come by these attributes naturally. We strive to reach this goal through starving, constant dieting, workouts, and coloring our hair. Many of us make our decisions based on the expectations of our lovers, mates, families, or friends. We have worn our hair a certain length or style because "he liked it that way." We have dieted extensively to achieve the waif-like appearance so popular in the media today. We have strived for perfection because it is the only way we feel we can be accepted and truly loved! How sad is this? We spend years of our lives trying to be something we are not and cannot achieve. As a result, we lose the joy of living. We don't know how to love and accept ourselves! I certainly don't think we should be disinterested in improving our appearance; however, I feel beauty, love, acceptance, and contentment comes from within ourselves. When we feel beautiful and loved on the inside, this message is transmitted to the outside world. We radiate a natural glow. Until we have achieved the ability to love others, including ourselves, all else is fake. This dissatisfaction and self-hatred prevents us from being the best we can be and certainly what God created us to be!

I had been no different. I had wasted precious years trying to be something I wasn't. I had dieted most of my adult life, striving to achieve the "perfect" weight. Once I reached what I thought was the magic number, I maintained it for less than a week! It was totally unrealistic. I had worn long hair because my fiancé preferred it. After he left me, I believed I wasn't good enough to meet someone to marry so I read one self-help book after another trying to figure out what was wrong. Since I didn't have a boyfriend, it seemed proof positive that I was lacking something. All my friends were married or about to be, but my fiancé backed out at the last minute and left me standing at the altar. *What's wrong with me? What am I missing?* The diagnosis of cancer and the prospect of losing a breast prompted all of my former uncertainties to return. I was consumed with negative and unworthy feelings.

The process of questioning who I was and what I represented continued for weeks. *I thought I resolved all this before. Why are these thoughts haunting me again? Maybe I should just go ahead and die and it would all be over!* Eventually, through many hours of prayer, share group discussions, and talks with friends and family members, the truth emerged. I knew I was a strong person by nature and had a deep faith in the Lord. I reminded myself what I knew was true: Jesus loved me as I was. I also knew I loved myself. I was reassured Jesus would help me through this huge hurdle and I would come out of the crisis as a whole and complete person. In time, I realized I was more than a body part! In and of itself, a breast was nothing and I accepted the fact that I could live without mine! What was most important was life itself. So, I had my mastectomy and surrendered my breast.

A dear friend, Trisha, came from Michigan to stay for ten days. She arrived before my surgery and stayed until my Mother's arrival ten days later. She watched the house and cared for my dogs. While I was in the hospital, she visited me twice daily and brought my mail and phone messages. Her support was so special! What I loved and appreciated was the way in which she decided to help. When she learned of my cancer and pending surgery, she made plans immediately to come. There was no doubt she wanted to support me during my crisis. When I asked if she was sure, her answer was simple. "You would do this, if the tables were turned. I can be there and I will." And she was. What a blessing her friendship was!

My surgery was uneventful and without complications. The first night post-op was one of sleeping and taking my pain shots every four hours. I remembered the nurses emptying the drains and administering another injection. Everything else was a blur. The second day, my appetite returned and, despite the dressings and two drains, I felt fairly good. I had even looked at the incision and was reassured to find it was neither offensive nor frightening. The day went well except for the fact I allowed myself too many visitors. By early evening, I was thoroughly exhausted. By the third day, I was adjusting exceptionally well. Trisha and I spent several hours that evening listening to comedy tapes by Carl Hurley, a Kentucky humorist. This was the best medicine I could have had. His tapes were hilarious and we laughed uncontrollably, until our sides ached and tears rolled down our faces. We were loud, raucous, and disruptive to the normally subdued hospital unit. I thought the nurses would ask us to be quiet, but no one said a word. Much later, they told me they could hear my laughter from the nursing station that evening. It was a positive sign because they realized laughter was an important factor in the healing process. They were pleased I was doing so well and never considered telling me to be more reserved— as if that would have made a difference!

The next morning, Sunday, was when I expected to be discharged. When a doctor came to check on me, he said nothing about my leaving. I had to speak up and raise the issue. Unfortunately, my regular surgeon was gone for the day and this physician was covering. He made it very clear he was in charge and would make all the decisions. His arrogance and unwillingness to work in developing a discharge plan angered me. I wanted to be home and didn't see any medical reason to stay. Anticipating I would question him further, he informed me I could only go home with one drain and since I had two, it was clearly not possible. I asked if we could remove one, to which he replied adamantly, "No." It was obvious I was not going to win that argument, so I decided to back off and approach him with a topic that might produce more satisfying results.

I asked about the lab report on the lymph nodes. He said he didn't know if it had been returned, but would check. I was feeling rather apprehensive as it seemed nothing was going my way. I wondered if it was a bad omen to ask. *Is it more bad news? I have to know this answer!* About five minutes later, one of the nurses came bouncing in my room with a broad smile on her face. She informed me all sixteen lymph nodes removed were negative!

I screamed and yelled, "Yes!"

Sixteen chances taken and sixteen signs of health and healing! God had spoken and I was truly ecstatic! Trisha, the nurses, and I celebrated that evening and it turned out to be a wonderful time. I didn't even mind staying one more night.

On Monday morning, when my regular surgeon returned, one of the drains was pulled without any hesitation and I was discharged by 10:00 A.M.

Hospitals have their place and I certainly had the very best care, but there is something wonderfully soothing about being in my own house. I have always felt peace and tranquility at home and would rather be in it than anywhere else. Besides, I missed my dogs tremendously and was looking forward to seeing them. My homecoming was just as glorious as I had anticipated. The dogs showered me with affection! They didn't care how I looked or what I had been through. They surrounded me with unconditional love and couldn't get enough of my attention. The feeling was mutual. I loved being with them, too.

I rested for most of the next two days. Trisha took care of everything, including going to the airport to pick up my mother, who was flying in from Arizona. Mom had planned to stay with me for the next month. Basically, I spent my time sleeping and/or going to doctor's appointments. The second drain stayed in for over three weeks and proved to be extremely uncomfortable. Because of it, I couldn't find a good position in which to sleep at night, and the slightest movement of any kind was extremely painful. Since the amount of drainage was quite significant, it was better to keep it so the fluids wouldn't collect excessively. If that happened, a syringe would have to be inserted. Even as a nurse, I found that thought rather horrifying and knew I didn't want to go down that path, so I kept the drain in.

After seven days, the drainage site became infected and my pain increased. Any movement created sharp, stabbing pains. One of the newer, expensive antibiotics was ordered, which increased my discomfort, as I don't handle that class of drugs very well. However, after several days, the pain subsided and I began to feel better. It wasn't until the end of the third week that the drain was finally removed. Once that happened, I felt normal again. The most wonderful thing was being able to take a simple shower. Being able to move without being attached to tubes gave me a sense of freedom that was exhilarating!

From that point forward, I never really felt "sick," but still had a long way to go in my recovery. I was severely limited with my arm movements and needed assistance daily. It wasn't unusual to get stuck in the midst of dressing and I literally could not move until my mother intervened. There was a constant feeling of "thickness" under my arm. It felt as though I was walking around with a large wad of cotton stuck in my armpit, which was a very strange sensation. Another part of the underarm area was numb and didn't seem like it was mine. Touching my axillary area was like having an "out of body" experience. Intellectually, I knew I was touching myself. Physically, I felt nothing.

As the days passed, there were sharp, shooting pains in my underarm and I was told to expect these impulses to continue for several months to a year. The nerve endings were trying to readjust. Driving my car was a major effort. The act of putting my car in gear, even though I drove an automatic, required me to stretch the tendons and muscles in my right arm. Turning the steering wheel replicated that same motion, so they both hurt tremendously. Lifting my arm was equally as exhausting as well as painful because of the extreme tightness from the incision. Nevertheless, I exercised my arm religiously so I could regain the full range of motion.

The most helpful exercise was to walk my fingers up the wall as I stood sideways to it. This action allowed the muscles to stretch and eased some of the tightness while providing support for my tired, aching arm. At each visit, my surgeon challenged me by asking for a demonstration of what I could do. He never seemed satisfied with my progress and always asked for more. As frustrating as it was, it also gave me the impetus to keep going when I felt tired and thought I couldn't do any better. He admitted he was pushing me because the sooner I was able to move my arm as normally as I could before my surgery, the easier it would be in the long run.

During my recovery, I experienced phantom pains, which is a phenomenon that occurs when one loses a body part. Even though that body part is missing, there is the sensation of an itch or pain and it seems like the lost body part still exists. Most often, I felt an itch on my nipple that I wanted to scratch, but there was neither a nipple nor a breast. I didn't expect this to happen.

During week three of my recovery, my brother flew in from Texas. It was my sister-in-law's suggestion. Both my mother and brother helped with chores around the house and yard because I was unable to do much. The best part of the visit was the time we had to reflect on my cancer, its meaning to each of us, our feelings about death and dying, and what our preferences were, if and when we died. Since my father had been ill most of my life, my parents and I had numerous family discussions about what should happen if we died. My brother, on the other hand, was in the Air Force during this time, so he had missed our family meetings; therefore, he knew nothing of my mother's or my preferences. We didn't know his either. In fact, the only discussions we had shared about death were those decisions that had to be made upon my father's passing, eight years earlier. Since that time, there had been no further conversation.

Now, with my surgery, the door opened to revisit the issue. Our talks yielded interesting surprises, in both directions. For example, I learned he had purchased a burial site for me because I was single. In fact, he had obtained enough mausoleum vaults for our family so we could be together. This information was unexpected!

Our time together yielded many other surprises and it turned out to be a very special time. I realized how lucky I was to have him for my brother. I reflected on how fortunate it was to attend college together. Despite our age difference of five years, it was that shared experience which brought us closer. The friendship and love that developed and strengthened during college, along with the blood ties as a small family, have been sustained over the years. It helped us view each other as true friends and confidantes.

As I moved toward full recovery and regaining the strength and movement in my arm, I felt my life was transitioning well. I believed I was going to be back on track shortly and was able to relax again.

For the first time in many months, my emotional state and physical condition improved significantly. It was then I realized God had definitely been guiding me and there was no reason to think He would not continue to do the same.

I felt my guardian angel, Frieda, had indeed been present in my surgery and was also watching over me.

I believed God was telling me I was going to be okay by the fact that the sixteen lymph nodes were clear. Indeed, they were all very positive signs, but little did I know God wasn't finished yet.

My Spiritual Lesson:

As a believer in Jesus, I am assured of an eternal life. That is a wonderful promise that awaits me, but in the interim, I am required to live in the earthly body I possess.

Sometimes our bodies make us groan and complain, especially when we are in the throes of an illness or pain, but that is also when I realized my present life was not all there was. There is a life after death and I will have a glorified body!

Knowing I will live with God, forever, in a place that has no pain or suffering helped me deal with the realities I was facing.

This knowledge gave me strength to move forward, but it didn't eliminate my fears and anxieties. When I learned the lymph nodes were clear, it was a positive sign. It meant I had more years to live! Honestly, as exciting as it can be to think about living in heaven, I still wanted to enjoy life in the present, even if it meant living in a damaged earthly tent.

"So we are always of good courage. We know that while we are at home in the body we are away from the Lord, for we walk by faith, not by sight. Yes, we are of good courage, and we would rather be away from the body and at home with the Lord. So, whether we are at home or away, we make it our aim to please Him." (2 Corinthians 5:6-9, NIV)

THE 6th SIGN: THREE-SIDED ROOMS AND OTHER ODDITIES

"For since the creation of the world God's invisible qualities—His eternal power and divine nature—have been clearly seen, being understood from what has been made, so that people are without excuse." (Romans 1:20, NIV)

One night, a week before my surgery, I had a very vivid dream. When I awakened, I had a hard time distinguishing between the dream and reality. I shook my head in disbelief and wonderment at its vividness because I could recall each detail of the dream so clearly. Throughout the day, I continued to reflect on it. I was unable to shake it from my consciousness. Since it had overtaken my mind, I decided to write it down with the plan to analyze it later.

Although I had previously dabbled in dream interpretation, I didn't do it with any regularity nor was I an expert. It was something that was generally more fun than serious, but I also knew when I experienced stressful situations in the past, my dreams often yielded information that could benefit me. I was aware dreams in the Bible were one of the most significant ways in which God communicated with others; therefore, it made me wonder if this was a message from God. I thought an analysis of the dream might provide valuable insight into my current struggles and help with my reintegration process. Additionally, honestly, the dream intrigued me. I believed it was to teach me a lesson.

Over the next months, my dream life was very active. At least, it was much more noticeable to me. The dreams were far more vivid than ever, and they stayed foremost in my mind. I was convinced God was trying to communicate through these dreams so I wrote them down and tried to interpret the messages I was getting.

I found the process of dream interpretation to be enlightening. In each of the situations, the dreams seemed like they were revealing some truth about my life and/or the struggles I was facing. They all related to my soul search.

My interpretations are solely my own.

I never talked with anyone who did this professionally, so I am not sure if someone with more experience in dream interpretation would come to the same conclusions.

Nevertheless, what follows are a few of the more significant dreams and my analyses.

The House Dream:

I had just completed renovating my house and it was exactly the way I wanted, both inside and outside. It was absolutely perfect! However, as soon as the work was finished, I no longer wanted to live in the house and immediately put it up for sale. I talked with a Realtor about buying an older home on a large hill behind my current home. It was one I had admired for quite some time and always thought I wanted to live in it. Before making a final decision, I asked to tour the house.

As we walked through the rooms, I realized they were all triangular. How odd was that? I commented about the three-sided shape of the rooms and the Realtor replied, "Oh, that is what makes this house so unique! That it's special character! You will love it, in time."

She was anxious to show me the family room, which she thought I would love. When we entered that room, I was overwhelmed with its size. It felt equivalent to a huge exhibition hall! My Realtor saw my reaction and commented, "What a wonderful room in which to entertain."

Then I noticed an extremely large, antique wooden table in the middle of the room. It was painted in a lovely shade of peach and was gorgeous. I was particularly impressed with the massiveness of the turned legs and instantly fell in love with it.

"This table is absolutely beautiful!" I said.

My realtor replied, "The table comes with the house, so that is why you have to buy this home. This is the only room that could hold a table of this size!"

My Dream Interpretation:

The renovated house represented my body. I had just taken care of a long-term health problem with my hysterectomy and felt wonderful! With my chronic pain gone, I felt like a new person. I was looking forward to getting in good physical shape and being able to exercise again. Then came the diagnosis of cancer that shook me to my core! The cancer was represented in the dream by wanting to get rid of the house (my body) because it wasn't perfect. It was filled with cancer and I didn't want any part of it.

The new house represented my new body.

The triangular-shaped rooms were the shape of my chest minus one breast. Indeed, I felt I would be unique and develop character because of my mastectomy experience, but I felt damaged. Even though my earthly tent was not the same, I realized God would repair it and make me whole.

I believed my future was represented by the large family room in the new house. Its expansiveness meant I had a full life ahead. I had a future—not death—and it was filled with great abundance! The peach table with the wooden legs represented the fact I would have all the strength and stamina I needed to handle my upcoming struggles. It represented everything wonderful and good in this world. The color peach (my favorite color) represented peace, tranquility, hope, and goodness in my life. I believed those qualities would be present in the years ahead and my life would be filled with joy and love.

I believed this dream was a message from God. Through it, I felt He was offering me hope again when I had little. He gave me assurance when I was faltering in my trust of Him. He provided me with a vision of tomorrow. Most of all, He was there to provide the strength and assistance I needed to continue on my healing journey.

About five weeks post-op, I walked to the mailbox one day, wearing shorts and a simple T-shirt without a bra. As I looked down to examine my mail, I suddenly realized my dream had been very accurate.

I was triangularly-shaped! Without one of my breasts, I had a distinct, three-sided view, when I looked down at my chest. I laughed out loud at the discovery and shook my head in amazement. Then I said softly, "Lord, you do know it all, don't you?" I delighted in His sense of humor and the manner in which He had revealed my new reality. I chuckled to myself as I returned to the house and smiled when I thought about His presence in my life.

The Surgery Dream:

I just completed having surgery in a very large, university-type of hospital. During my recovery, no one paid any attention to me. It was as if I was invisible. Nothing I said or did was taken seriously. People talked to me and asked what I needed, but they never provided the assistance I requested. I was simply ignored. My pleas for help went unanswered.

The Surgery Dream Interpretation:

This dream represented the feelings I experienced after moving from Michigan and leaving my church and support system. I relocated to Kentucky, where I knew no one. I had hoped to rely on my Michigan friends to be my support for a while, but that's not what happened. I felt incredibly alone and expected my friends to keep in touch, especially after my cancer diagnosis. Instead, they had forgotten me when I needed their support more than ever. I was upset and hurt. Not only was I disappointed with them, but I was angry with God for bringing me to Kentucky and having to deal with the cancer. This dream was like a slap in the face.

Suddenly, I realized how ridiculous it was to expect my Michigan friends to be my support system. Rather, it was time to grieve my loss and move on. If I chose not to do this, I was creating barriers toward building new relationships in Kentucky. I needed to start living in the present and stop focusing on what used to be.

The dream also revealed it was time to end a long-distance relationship I had been trying to maintain. The arrangement was not working and I had been very dissatisfied for a while. We had moved from dating one another to a friendship status, but that yielded nothing. Now, it was almost a year later and our relationship had gotten more problematic. When we were together, I felt disappointment and anger and could hardly wait until he left. It was fostering feelings of inadequacy and insignificance.

Once I ended it, I felt an immediate sense of relief and a boost to my self-esteem.

There were other areas of my life the dream tapped into as well—particularly, my relationships. I thought about boundaries that had been crossed and reviewed all of my existing relationships, to determine what needed to be kept versus what to put aside. I used this dream to explore how I was relating to others and decided to make changes in moving forward with new relationships.

The Furniture Dream:

I came home to find my golden retriever had chewed and ripped up the furniture in my living room. Both of my upholstered chairs and sofa were totally demolished. The fabric and padding lay in shreds on the floor. I felt shocked and angry. I believed he should be punished for his wrongful behavior, but I didn't know how.

The Furniture Dream Interpretation:

This dream spoke of the body mutilation I was experiencing with losing a breast. Both the dream scenario and the mastectomy were things over which I had no control, but they were also situations in which I felt a great deal of anger and despair. However, the time had come to accept the changes. The only way I could learn to love and accept myself was to give up my negativity. This also meant giving up the anger I felt toward God for what I believed was abandonment.

If I continued focusing on these feelings, I was impairing my chances for a complete healing. It would also change me in ways I didn't want and would negatively affect all future relationships as well as my own self-esteem. I needed to move toward a state of health, which meant accepting my brokenness. It was time to acknowledge that each of us has gaping wounds that need to be healed. I was no different than others who have been through the same experience. I could offer my brokenness to Jesus and rest in His love. In return, He would offer me mercy and wholeness. I knew His love was genuine and something I could count on without question. If I used His love as my compass, I could not go wrong. I wanted to reach out toward others and share His love with others.

The Hotel Room Dream:

I was staying in a hotel where people kept coming into my room to use the elevator. I was puzzled why this was necessary. I tried to lock the door, but it wouldn't work and the steady stream of people continued. Initially, I felt discouraged and depressed, but then I grew to accept it, even though I didn't understand it.

The Hotel Room Interpretation:

This dream represented the drain that I had to keep in for three weeks following the surgery. As much as I wanted it removed and resisted the surgeon's orders to keep it, I finally acknowledged the amount of fluids that continued to collect justified its use. That was when it made sense. I moved into a role of acceptance and decided to "go with the flow."

My depression and discouragement began to dissipate. I finally took responsibility for making the decision to have a mastectomy because, after all, I had choices. So, I really did have control! I was not powerless. I had chosen the best path for healing, but realized I could not do it alone. It was also time to trust God because He has the ultimate control over my life. "Let go and let God!"

The Walk Dream:

I was with a large group of people who were on a spiritual retreat. We were supposed to go on a two-mile walk, in groups of four. At designated points, we stopped for a few minutes to discuss what each of the settings represented in our walk with Jesus. The first point was a forest of evergreens, with four to six rows of trees in every direction. The second stop was a large, campus-like setting, with an expanse of green grass on rolling hills. The third point was a flower garden filled with roses. At that setting, I focused intently on one particular rose. While I watched, the rose slowly unfolded before me. I was in awe of what was happening.

The Walk Dream Interpretation:

This dream provided insight about my relationships. The forest was my job and I believed I was being told to look for Jesus among the people with whom I worked.

Although I was in a middle of a large healthcare organization and was still pretty new to the facility, I realized there were many people who truly cared. I had an amazing number of coworkers who shared their concerns and prayers. On a daily basis, they offered support in ways I never expected.

I realized I could look to them, rather than allowing myself to feel alone and isolated. Also, I knew God was present and I needed to turn to Him.

The large campus setting took on the meaning of a "clean slate." I believed I was being given a chance to start over and, in fact, was being asked to live in a very different way.

Finally, the rose represented life itself. I believed I had more years ahead and I needed to be more aware of God's presence. Indeed, there was beauty and God's love being shown through the people, nature, and the events that were occurring.

I had to allow myself to experience the fullness of each moment and appreciate the precious gift life truly is.

The Babies Dream:

My former Michigan pastor and another female friend had just delivered some babies. They were in a competitor's hospital and I was on my way to visit them.

However, in order to see them, I had to go to a "major" floor, located on the seventh level.

When I arrived at this floor, I was told I would have to give each patient an injection before I would be permitted to visit with my friends.

The Babies Dream Interpretation:

This dream spoke of the opportunity for a new kind of life with Jesus, which was symbolized by the birth of the babies. Before I could appreciate and experience the joy from it, I would have to overcome some unique challenges. Spiritual growth with transformation was never a simple task. It required total commitment and discipline in all areas of my life. It also meant keeping my eyes on God's goals rather than on mine.

Interestingly, the number seven took on some significance of its own.

In the Bible, seven is a number associated with perfection or completion. I was on sick leave for seven weeks for the surgery and recovery. In addition, the total amount of time from diagnosis and surgery to the last chemo treatment was seven months! From my view, this was what I needed for complete healing. God was watching over me.

The issue of the competitor's hospital probably represented the fact I was in a "foreign territory" as I traveled through the entire cancer experience. Even though I am a nurse, oncology was not my area of expertise, so I had to re-educate myself. Of course, my perspective was firsthand as the patient, which made my experience different from being a student in the classroom, or a nurse working inside a hospital unit.

Where did the emphasis on "major" come in? I believed it was because I was making a huge change in how I was living. I was in such a dark valley during my treatment that the only way I could survive was to rely on Jesus to get me through each day.

The injection represented Jesus. I had to insert more of Him in my life on a daily basis. Yes, that is a powerful injection!

The Prisoner Dream:

I was being held as a prisoner in a room and was trying to find a way to escape. I looked out the window and realized there was a body on the window ledge. When I examined it, I suddenly became aware it was someone I knew, but couldn't identify who it was. Yet, I knew it was very familiar. Unfortunately, the body was dead. Suddenly, the body turned over by itself and fell from the ledge as I watched in horror.

The Prisoner Dream Interpretation:

The body on the ledge represented me. If I allowed the fear of and anger toward cancer to rule my life from that point forward, then I would become imprisoned in a hell of my own choosing. This would allow me to "die" on many levels other than just a physical death.

However, if I faced my feelings and dealt with them by relying on Jesus, I could experience freedom and love.

I was encouraged by the dream to take an active role in my recovery process. This meant healing was possible, physically, by getting involved in all aspects of my care and treatment. At the same time, healing had to occur on many levels beyond the physical side.

The more important area was my spiritual self. I acknowledged it was vitally important to turn myself over to Jesus and allow Him full control. Trust was essential. Otherwise, I could literally "roll over and die," like the body on the ledge. Living without Jesus meant I was not living.

The Trip Dream:

A co-worker of mine was going with the hospital's administrative team to a conference in California. Since she was not a vice-president, I asked how it was possible that she was able to go. She identified herself as their assistant. The group would be gone for a period of 60 days. She asked if she could borrow my sewing machine to take, so she could complete the various tasks being asked of her.

The Trip Dream Interpretation:

I believed this dream helped deal with the guilt I had for being on sick leave. With the combined sick leaves from my two surgeries (the hysterectomy and the mastectomy), I actually missed a total of 60 work days. I had never been off for any length of time due to an illness. Yet, here I was, at a new job, taking the second substantial sick leave in less than two years! I felt embarrassed with needing this amount of time and wondered if the hospital regretted hiring me.

The sewing machine represented the process of putting myself back together (physically, emotionally, and spiritually). It was clearly a reconstruction of myself that I had to achieve before I could return to work and be effective in my job.

My Friends Dream:

I was at a church gathering with my Michigan friends. As I came out of one building and was about to cross the street to another building, I saw my friend's three young toddlers sitting on the street curb. The children's grandmother came along, took the hand of the little girl, and they walked away.

I was just about to escort the two young boys across the street when their father walked up and grabbed my hand.

I questioned why he was kidding around rather than tending to his boys.

He replied, "Their mother is coming and they can wait for her. Right now, you need me more and I am going to help you." Then he took my hand and escorted me away.

The Friends Dream Interpretation:

I believed this dream was telling me that friends would play a very key role in my recovery. Since I had always assumed the role of caretaker, I found it difficult to accept help or assistance because it had always made me feel weak. As a result, I usually tried to avoid such situations.

Now, I realized I needed to change this attitude. By allowing others to care for me, I was clearly giving up control. This was a lesson I really needed to learn.

Not only was it an acceptable thing to do, it allowed Jesus to reveal Himself through my friends' actions.

My Spiritual Lesson:

God uses many avenues to communicate. Of course, scripture and prayer are the most common. It was amazing how the same Bible passage spoke to me differently each day, depending upon what was happening in my life. Some days, a scripture would jump out from the page and it was so obvious how it applied. Other days, I had to search for His Word.

In addition to the dreams, I also felt there were messages through nature, the people I met, and the events that occurred in my daily life. Each day was filled with an exciting surprise, if I was willing to look for it. It became like a scavenger hunt! I looked forward to what the message of the day was!

"The heavens declare the glory of God; the skies proclaim the work of his hands. Day after day, they pour forth speech; night after night, they reveal knowledge. They have no speech, they use not words; no sound is heard from them. Yet their voice goes out into all the earth, their words to the ends of the world." (Psalms 19:1-4, NIV)

"May these words of my mouth and this meditation of my heart be pleasing in Your sight, Lord, my Rock and my Redeemer." (Psalms 19:14, NIV)

THE 7th SIGN: CARRIED BY THE LIGHT

"The Lord is my light and my salvation—who shall I fear? The Lord is the stronghold of my life—of whom shall I be afraid?" (Psalms 27:1, NIV)

I have been blessed with the ability to think positively and expect the best outcome in what I do. I think it is the greatest strength I possess. Even though it generally works to my advantage, sometimes when I am feeling down and discouraged, the great contrast in my mood can make those dark days seem even darker. Fortunately, those days don't come often, nor do they last long. For the most part, I have been thankful for my optimistic attitude about life. I believe it was both taught by and inherited from my parents.

My father always thought good would prevail, despite his numerous illnesses, surgeries, and general ill health. He had complete faith in his physicians and recovered quickly from thirteen major surgeries. He engaged easily with others and his sense of humor made him appear healthy, even when he wasn't feeling well. The unfortunate part was the fact he couldn't share that same life-giving energy and enthusiasm within our family. Mostly, we saw the gloom that resulted from him not feeling well and it was a great burden to bear. When the seldom seen days arrived wherein he felt genuinely good and whole, he was truly a vibrant and loving man. Being with him was delightful while his sense of "wellness" lasted. Sadly, it never sustained any of us, especially him. I knew this was not his fault, so I was never angry with him for his poor health. Instead, I felt inordinately sad he could not live the kind of life he deserved.

From my mother, I learned about the importance of maintaining a positive outlook. She lived in a world filled with constant trips to the hospital, endless medical bills, and a sense of living each day on the edge of a great precipice. It was only after my father's death that I saw a new side of my mother emerge, which I'm sure had been hidden with the burden of caring for him. After a year of grieving my father's death (and the loss of a 48-year marriage), she blossomed into a confident and outgoing woman who was exuberant about life. The weight had been lifted from her shoulders. She truly demonstrated her joy in living and set a goal of reaching the age of 125! She exuded a new sense of happiness. In her year of grieving, her faith had grown exponentially as she re-ignited her relationship with Jesus. Laughter was a common part of each day and her personality became totally alive. I came to value how she managed the hardships she experienced in life, including her personal experience with colon cancer. She continued to be my best friend and my foundation until her passing in 2008 at the age of 92!

It was my usual optimism—along with some naiveté—that led me to believe I had stopped the spread of cancer. Based on my surgeon's recommendations, I thought the worst was over! I believed surgery alone was sufficient. Why I never entertained the idea of chemotherapy, I will never know. Denial is a wonderful defense mechanism and it was effective, even though my nursing knowledge should have countered that belief. When my hormone sensitivity tests came back with unusual results, I was referred to an oncologist regarding the next level of treatment. I was flabbergasted! More treatment? Oh, no, that cannot be! Hormone tests are routinely performed with breast cancer and the results determine the treatment regimen. Often, the test yields the same results for the progesterone and estrogen; however, mine were different. The progesterone was positive and the estrogen was negative. This mixed picture confused the experts. The lab completing the tests recommended a course of chemotherapy. Since this was their specialty, my surgeon agreed, but deferred to the oncologist. I was deflated, confused, and frightened! Due to the negative chemo experiences of friends and family, I was very reluctant to accept chemo and was willing to do anything to avoid it!

Much of my fear of chemotherapy came from watching my mother adjust to her regimen with colon cancer. Since chemo was in its infancy at that time (the early 1970s), my mother's treatment protocols were very crude and actually quite experimental in nature. There were only a small number of cancer drugs, and all were new and basically unproven.

Today, Mother's treatment protocol would be considered archaic because so much more is known. Nonetheless, my mother endured intravenous chemo on a weekly basis for seven long years! Life was truly awful. Three or four days out of each week were lost because she was unable to function. She stayed in bed most of those days. She couldn't eat without feeling ill and experienced the ever-present nausea, headaches, and almost constant dizziness. This pattern remained the same for seven years. The doctors had no empathy and offered little relief for her symptoms. In the midst of her agony and discomfort, she somehow managed to educate herself about the importance of specific foods, vitamins, and minerals. She established her own nutritional protocols. The changes in her diet, along with the combinations of specific supplements, finally gave her some relief. She also learned that, if she ate certain foods at distinct times, her side effects from the chemo were lessened. In this way, she was able to tolerate her lengthy treatment. I know this was not easy to endure but, with the help of God, she recovered and was free of cancer for the next 28 years! Amazing!

Armed with the knowledge of Mother's experience and cloaked in fear, I met with an oncologist who was highly regarded in the community.

As expected, his recommendation was a six-month course of chemotherapy. He was definitely in agreement with the lab's suggestion. I told him my veins were terrible. That, he countered, could be handled with a portacath insertion.

Then he informed me, "I can guarantee you will lose your hair, but it will grow back."

His comments hit me like a brick wall. The sting lingered, even after he excused himself to check on my lab reports.

While he was out of the room, I told my friend who accompanied me that I couldn't do it. I didn't want to lose my hair and didn't believe I could handle all the side effects. She had been through chemo herself and tried to reassure me.

"You can do it for six months and it will lengthen your life."

When the oncologist returned, he confirmed what he had said earlier. He recommended we begin chemo immediately and wanted to know my decision NOW.

I explained I needed time to consider the options.

He asked, "What are you thinking?"

I replied, "I don't want to do it!"

He asked, "Why?"

I explained I didn't want to lose my hair.

Immediately, his retort was, "That is the stupidest thing I have ever heard! I said hair will grow back. Do you want to risk your life for your hair?"

I couldn't speak. I was about to explode and wanted to leave his office. How arrogant! I can't stand how he is talking to me! Who does he think he is? I need a different doctor who understands me!

Then he informed me that research had established chemo was more effective when it was initiated within six weeks of surgery. It was now seven days away from that mark, so there was no time to waste. He tried to set up an appointment for the portacath surgery for the following Monday, but I refused. I just wanted out of there! I had to leave before I said or did something I regretted.

We ended the appointment with him giving me the weekend to consider my options. He then demanded I call on Monday with my decision.

I left the office in a daze. I couldn't believe what I had heard! In my mind, it was absolutely the worst news and sent me into a state of panic and shock! I left the doctor's appointment and went straight to have my hair cut and colored. As soon as I walked into the hair salon, everyone knew something was wrong. I burst into tears as I told them what had happened. Immediately, both staff and clients gathered round to give me hugs. I shared my fears and uncertainty about chemo and told them I was considering not having it. Then the owner of the salon thought about another client who had recently been treated for breast cancer. She suggested talking to her before making a decision. After thinking about the offer, I agreed.

That woman and I spoke for forty-five minutes on the phone. Her experience was not as awful as my mother's, which was encouraging. She offered to be a support, even though we had not met. She even was willing to accompany me to the chemo treatments, if I decided to go that route! I was amazed at her offer. Nonetheless, her comments soothed my anxieties and I was able to compose myself. Unfortunately, this composure was brief.

Once my hair was cut and the color was processing, I burst into tears. I suddenly realized this was probably the last time I would be able to color my hair.

What will I do? I know there is gray at the roots, so what is my hair going to be like if I cannot color it? How will I handle having no hair? How ugly will I look? Will I be bald? I didn't think I could handle any of that and my former fears and anxieties quickly returned. By that point, I wanted to escape from the world. Let me go home and feel sorry for myself! I want to disappear from the earth! Please, Lord, just let me die now!

During the drive home, my thoughts immediately focused on my mother's reaction to the news. She was four days away from returning to Arizona and I anticipated she would be very upset. I expected her to share in my shock and offer to change her reservations so she could help.

When I told her the recommendation, she reacted with such calmness that I was confused.

"Well, you just need to do it. I am sorry you have to, but you can handle it."

Talk about shock! I thought she was cold and insensitive about the whole matter. Even my own mother has no empathy! What's wrong with this picture?

I hated my mother's reaction. I expected better and she disappointed me greatly.

After saying what she did, she excused herself to the bedroom to pack her belongings. I stood there, aghast. What just happened? She may have cried in the bedroom. I honestly don't know. I had expected her to say, "I wish I could do this instead of you." However, she said nothing. Based on her past experience, I don't think she considered that option. What I know is she wasn't about to share any sadness. Mother told me she chose life. In this situation, she clearly expected me to do the same.

The weekend was horrible. I cried most of the time and felt like my world had come to an abrupt end for the second time! It seemed the Mack truck, which hit me when I was told I had cancer, had turned around and was coming back to strike again. I wanted to run away and hide. I wanted my easy life back— the one that existed before the nightmares began. I had taken my good health for granted and I wished I could relive those days and appreciate what I had. I was ready to bargain with God. If you give me back my former life, I will never argue with you again! I thought I could convince God to meet my demands, but they were promises I knew I couldn't keep. God, I'll do everything you want me to do. That was unlikely! My intentions were good, but I am a sinful human and there was no way I could follow through with what I was saying. God knew that, but it sure sounded good. I was ready to give up anything in order to turn the clock back and live those years over again.

There was little conversation between Mother and me about the chemo. Her expectation was simply that I would make the same choice she did. My brother agreed with Mother. I tried to explain how unsure I was about doing it, but no one wanted to hear it. There was no consideration for my preference. I did NOT want chemo! I was struggling with whether I had the fortitude to handle it. I wasn't sure I did. Nevertheless, after much prayer and consternation, I decided to follow through with the proposed plan.

When Monday arrived, I called and arranged both for the portacath surgery and my first chemo treatment on Friday.

Mother returned to Arizona on Tuesday. Only once before leaving did she say she wished she could be there for my first treatment. She never offered to change her plane reservations and I didn't ask. In retrospect, I think Mother welcomed the fact she could leave. Part of her wanted to be there, but I'm sure she really didn't want to face the big "C" again. It is possible the memories of her experience may have been more than she could have handled. Once my treatment was behind me, I was able to view this exchange differently. Her reaction made more sense. The sights and smells of chemo are very powerful and reliving it is not something one wants to re-experience. Mother was likely feeling this way, but may have been unable to express it, especially to me. At a later point, I shared my thoughts and her only response was a smile. That said it all. We were clearly on the same wavelength, but I asked God to forgive my short-sightedness.

I was placed on a program of one treatment with three drugs (Cytoxan, Methotrexate, and Fluorouracil AKA 5FU). These were given intravenously and then I had a week off before I received another treatment with two of the drugs. I had two weeks free before I repeated the pattern the next month. This regimen was to be six months (twelve treatments) in length.

A friend and her daughter came from Michigan for my initial chemo treatment. From the beginning, I vomited for several hours and felt lousy. I slept as much as I could or rested otherwise. My friends pampered me and it helped. By Sunday, I felt good enough to go out for dinner. I was starved and could actually eat my food without problems. I thought perhaps I had overreacted and maybe the chemo wasn't going to be so awful after all. For some reason, my denial was at work again. I didn't expect the treatment to get more difficult as the months passed. I should have known better!

After the second treatment in the first month, my hair began to fall out in huge handfuls. It was terrifying. There are no words to describe the horror of losing your hair. I burst into tears and sobbed uncontrollably. When I went out in the open air, the smallest breeze blew hair off my head. It was sheer terror! I smelled the chemo drugs in my urine and perspiration, and it was sickening. Everything had a metallic taste, but it was worse drinking pop from a can. I developed mouth ulcers and could hardly eat anything without great pain and discomfort. I vomited despite the fact they gave me the "wonder" drug, Zofran, which was supposed to lessen the nausea.

Mother offered a suggestion to alleviate my nausea and vomiting. She learned that sipping pineapple juice like soup was beneficial for her. She thought it might ease my discomfort, so I tried it. Amazingly, it worked! It was a miracle! It did everything she said it would and I was thankful for some relief. I relished the taste of the cold pineapple juice and found it soothed me enormously.

I also developed conjunctivitis in both eyes. The oncologist claimed it was not a side effect from the chemo. My ophthalmologist said it was.

A pattern quickly developed. In the weeks between the second treatment and the beginning of the next month's treatment, my eyes would burn, tear, and sting. It hurt to keep them open and it was nearly impossible to read anything or watch TV. This lasted approximately ten days to two weeks each month. Along with the conjunctivitis, I had a runny nose which was uncontrollable and very embarrassing. I walked around with a box of tissues to wipe my nose. It appeared as though I was coming down with a cold, but I never did develop one the entire time. I was truly miserable.

As I entered the third month of chemo, my misery increased. I complained to the oncologist and his nurse about the side effects from the Zofran. As soon as they administered it, I immediately developed diarrhea. This was a common reaction, and they told me to deal with it. However, my vision was also adversely affected. It was very painful keeping my eyes open while receiving the Zofran, but what was more disturbing was the strange pressure sensation I experienced.

It felt like something was forcing my eyes to bulge outward, as if they were being pushed out of the eye sockets. My doctor had never heard this complaint and looked at me with bewilderment and disbelief. His response frustrated me even more because it seemed like he didn't believe what I was saying. Regardless, he adjusted the Zofran dosage and increased the amount of fluids in which it was diluted. This relieved my immediate discomfort during the actual treatment but, routinely after the first treatment of each series, I vomited continuously for two full days.

I also started vomiting after the second and easier treatment each month. I hated doing this, but there was nothing that seemed to help or prevent it.

At that point, even the pineapple juice had lost its effectiveness. My oncologist said I was experiencing "anticipatory anxiety" and explained I was reacting in a negative way to the treatments even before coming to the center. He was correct.

I dreaded the treatment days.

I found them so overwhelming that just thinking about them would send my body into "shudders," so he prescribed Ativan, which I was to begin taking the evening before. Taking it every six hours allowed me to have three doses in my body before my treatment. I felt "buzzed" and not quite "all there," which allowed me to tolerate the treatment better. This accomplished the task of physically getting me into the physician's office and helped with my emotional response. The longer I waited in the reception area prior to my treatment, the more anxiety I experienced.

I developed a routine of arriving just in time to walk into the treatment area, which reduced my sense of panic. I was not only surprised, but felt disappointed with my reactions. As a psychiatric nurse, I thought I should be better equipped. After all, I knew how to deal with patients who suffered from anxiety. Why couldn't I do the same for myself? But it didn't work that way. I was as unable to help myself as a surgeon is unable to do surgery on himself. I was also not very tolerant or understanding of my own feelings. If people asked how they could help, I told them they could take a gun and shoot me, to relieve my misery. This, of course, shocked them, when they realized I wasn't kidding. They often didn't know how to respond and would laugh and say, "Now, Rita, it's not that bad." Or they would completely avoid me.

I wasn't suicidal, but I was caught up in my own misery.

My doctor and his nurse were the ones who kept reminding me I was a patient and shouldn't be placing such impossible demands on myself. They explained my reactions were normal and I needed to be more accepting of what I was experiencing. They frequently commented, "Chill out!" Honestly, it was good advice, but we all know just telling someone to do it doesn't make it happen.

Also during the third month of chemo, I met a woman who was going through the same treatment protocol. We talked while receiving our individual treatments one day. She reported experiencing no side effects. She did admit there was a period of 23 hours where she felt a little "hazy," but then all was well again. She found the treatments quite tolerable and had not lost even one hair!

Outwardly, I was very nice, but on the inside, a volcano was raging!

Even though we just met, I hated her like I have never hated anyone in my life. I wanted to scream at the top of my lungs. Lord, this is not fair! Why can't I have the same experience? What did I do to deserve this?

My anger with God was huge and something with which I had to deal daily. It was overwhelming.

When I was at home, I yelled and screamed at God. I called Him names and cussed Him out. I slammed things around and hit my fist into my pillow.

When I visited my doctor, I told him how much I hated all of this. Surprisingly, he would nod his head and tell me he understood, although I wasn't sure he did.

The person who received the brunt of my anger was the nurse who administered my chemo. Every time, I would tell her how much I hated and despised the treatments and how I didn't want to be there. She was very sweet and told me she understood. She apologized for poking me with the needles and said she was sorry I had to endure such pain and agony. I knew she felt bad, but there was nothing more she could do.

The wonderful gift she offered was the opportunity to allow me to express my feelings openly. I was never judged by her for anything, despite the fact that I said some pretty awful things and behaved poorly.

As the months passed, my anxiety level skyrocketed higher each month. My doctor was increasingly concerned both about my emotional and physical reactions. He told me if I couldn't handle the outpatient treatments, he would hospitalize me. I refused. He said he would keep me for four hours in the outpatient area while they gave me additional fluids, to reduce the risk of dehydration. I refused this as well. If I can't tolerate staying in the treatment area for two hours, how can I stay for four? Is this man crazy? Doesn't he know how difficult this is? I constantly fought the idea of ripping the IV lines from my body and running away. My entire body shook so badly that I felt like I was having a convulsion. I asked for a home health nurse to come to my house and do the treatments, but my oncologist wouldn't approve it because it was too dangerous. The chemo caused me to gain weight, but my oncologist kept accusing me of overeating. Nothing could have been further from the truth. At that point, after the first treatment of each series, I vomited endlessly for four days. I couldn't keep anything down and ran the risk of being severely dehydrated.

I understood my doctor's concerns, as I was dangerously on the edge.

Nothing seemed to help.

Furthermore, I couldn't sleep, so I was exhausted all the time. I was tired of not having any energy and not being able to handle simple daily chores. I couldn't find any comfortable positions because I suffered from an ever-present state of agitation and restlessness and couldn't figure out how to alleviate it. I dreaded going to the next treatment. I felt like I was going crazy. I thought about dying and believed it might have been a better alternative than what I was experiencing! I kept asking my mother how she did it for so long. She said she wanted to live. At that point, I wasn't sure what I wanted. I knew my treatments were my lifeline to wellness, but I didn't know what that meant any more. God, I'm not sure I want to live. This is a nightmare of my own choosing. Why are you making me go through this? I didn't believe I could make it to the end and wondered if I gave up now, what would it mean? I felt weak and wanted to walk away from everything.

I prayed fervently for Jesus to help me, but I didn't always feel His intervention and certainly didn't feel any relief. I had never felt so lost and alone in my life as I did on some of those days. I asked for prayers from everyone I knew. Both my Michigan and Kentucky churches had prayer watches and my share group also joined in. I leaned on friends and acquaintances like never before and tried to draw upon their strength to get through the long days and nights.

The last two months dragged on interminably. I thought they would never end nor did I believe I would survive. The very last month was the only time my blood count was so low that the treatments were delayed a week. When that happened, it made things worse. I thought I would die from sheer dread!

I had timed the treatments to know they were supposed to end on November 19th. However, due to that delay, I ended up having the final treatment the day before Thanksgiving.

When my last chemo ended, I literally yelled and screamed with total delight! Happy Holidays, Rita! I was certain everyone in the office suite (and perhaps on the whole floor) heard me yell! I hugged the nurse and everyone else. I couldn't believe I actually made it!

I AM FINISHED! YES, I AM DONE AND I AM STILL ALIVE! HALLELUJAH! THANK YOU, JESUS!

Once the treatments were completed, I told my friends I was partying for the next six weeks, since it coincided with the holidays of Thanksgiving, Christmas, and New Year's. And I did! Any opportunity to celebrate was pounced upon immediately. It started the very next day with Thanksgiving. I was invited over to a friend's house to join her family. Even though I didn't feel well and had no appetite, I wanted the company of others. Their family celebrated my success and it was a joyous occasion.

I wanted to celebrate everything. I was so happy! I am alive! My chemo is over! Thank you, Jesus!

My joy was bursting at the seams and I thought I couldn't contain myself. I was so appreciative of everything, regardless how big or small. I thanked the Lord for life!

I never expected to live through my experience of cancer, but I was carried by the light and finally reached it at the end of the tunnel!

My Spiritual Lesson:

Throughout the chemo, I tried to envision God's healing light flowing into my body while I received the IV fluids.

I used music, visualization exercises, and relaxation techniques to assist in this process, in addition to many prayers.

I imagined His light running like a river into my body and through my cells.

The light was extremely bright, warm, and oddly translucent, and it made me feel exceptionally good and surrounded in unconditional love. As the light came in contact with the cancer, the cells were destroyed and removed from my body by that river of light.

I felt close to Jesus for the time I visualized Him and His presence, but I couldn't always sustain that wonderful feeling to last throughout the length of each treatment. It was too easy to revert to the misery of my situation and allow myself to feel awful again. Regardless, I knew the chemo was God's own healing power and goodness entering my body. It was a sign He was helping to get well. He had carried me toward the light and had, once again, led me in the direction I needed to go. Once the chemo was finished, I understood more intimately the meaning of His mercy and grace.

"You, O Lord, keep my lamp burning; my God turns my darkness into light." (Psalms 18:28, NIV)

THE 8th SIGN: BROKEN, YET WHOLE

"Rather, as servants of God we commend ourselves in every way; in great endurance; in troubles, hardships and distresses; in beatings, imprisonments and riots; in hard work, sleepless nights and hunger; in purity, understanding, patience and kindness in the Holy Spirit and in sincere love; in truthful speech and in the power of God; with weapons of righteousness in the right hand and in the left, through glory and dishonor, bad report and good report; genuine, yet regarded as impostors, known, yet regarded as unknown; dying, and yet we live on; beaten and yet not killed; sorrowful, yet always rejoicing; poor, yet making many rich; having nothing, and yet possessing everything." (2 Corinthians 6:4-10, NIV)

Brokenness results from pain and no one asks for or wants to endure either! Why would anyone wish for an experience of suffering, hurt, or some kind of misfortune that causes an enormous amount of distress and agony?

Jesus chose to obey His Father and place himself in that position when He was on earth, but what about us? If we knew pain was in our future, would we eagerly volunteer? I doubt it. So, why does pain exist? Does it serve a purpose? What possible benefit could come of it? And then the real question—does it really make a difference, as to its kind? Pain is pain. It is something we want to avoid at any cost (perhaps even to the point of selling our soul to the devil himself)! Whether it is emotional or physical pain, it hurts. Sadly, it is part of our human condition. Regardless, when I entered into brokenness, I didn't want to experience any pain, nor did I want any part of being broken.

Brokenness, to me, included all the changes that altered everything from my actual body shape to my emotional state. Having only one breast made me lopsided. I felt like an oddity—different, but not in a good way. While at home, I could tolerate the asymmetry, but outside the home, I felt the need to appear "normal." This meant wearing a prosthesis so others would not suspect my deformity, but I found it heavy and unnatural. I disliked it. I felt ugly! I viewed myself as "damaged goods" and a fake!

Clothes fit differently, which was frustrating. Any garment with a fitted bustline required me to wear a prosthesis to make it fit properly. Without it, there would be awkward gaps in the material that just looked weird. I felt ridiculous. I could no longer wear anything that had spaghetti straps or was strapless because the bra that held my prosthesis had wide straps, which were needed to support its weight. Sadly, the pleasure of wearing sexy lingerie was taken away and I reverted to sleeping in old T-shirts. I felt awkward around my girlfriends if we were in a situation where I had to reveal my lopsided chest. What will they think of me? Will I look strange to them? However, I soon learned my friends did not view me as freakish. Instead, they were very loving and compassionate and did what they could to help me feel "normal."

I also felt broken because my identity as a woman was shattered. I wondered what this meant for future romantic relationships. I was still young and hoped I would meet that special guy, but now I questioned if he would accept me. If I don't have two breasts, how can he consider me attractive? Will I be rejected?

Did I make a mistake in not getting the simultaneous breast reconstruction? One of the main reasons I chose not to have any reconstructive surgery was because I had heard too many horror stories from others who regretted making that decision. I decided I would adjust better to my new reality by waiting until a later point for the surgery.

My initial plan was to wear a prosthesis for a year or two and then do the reconstructive surgery, but life unfolded differently.

Subsequent job changes caused a move to another state. One thing led to another and my surgery decision was delayed multiple times. I ended up wearing the prosthesis for about ten years! When I finally decided I was ready for reconstructive surgery, it took time to find a surgeon I could trust. My excitement began to build as I anticipated having the surgery. My first thought was that I would feel "whole" again and have two breasts like a "real" woman.

The surgery went well with the insertion of an implant. However, my recovery did not. I sustained an infection that resulted in two additional surgeries within the next eight months. Of course, the implant had to be removed. I was back at square one. My body required several months to recover, but my emotional status took longer. I had to deal with the disappointment that my surgery had failed along with my dream for restoration. At that point, I was done with surgery. I decided God was telling me it was time to accept who I had become. He loved me as I was and that is what He expected me to do as well.

I learned firsthand about suffering during my surgery and treatment series. For me, the suffering was both emotional and physical. There were many days when I thought I would never again know what it was like to feel "good." I knew pain and suffering were common when one traveled in the "valley of darkness," but I didn't want to experience it. I knew that was unrealistic, but it didn't matter—it is how I felt.

When we are at our lowest and think we cannot go on for another minute, we entertain drastic thoughts. I found myself questioning everything.

Why is this necessary? Why me, Lord? What can I do to bypass this hurdle? What do You want from me?

At this juncture of my illness, I entered the "bargaining" phase with God.

I never once viewed my cancer as punishment from God for a sin I committed or because I lacked a strong enough faith. Neither did I consider it the work of Satan, although I am convinced his forces exist in a great and real presence in our world today. Instead, I saw it as part of our human condition, resulting from Adam and Eve's actions in the Garden of Eden. Of one thing, I was sure—I felt a level of personal responsibility for having cancer! I should have taken better physical care of myself over the years. I should have eaten more well-balanced meals (making sure I consumed an adequate number of fruits and vegetables), exercised on a more consistent basis, and taken my vitamins and minerals daily. I was now very aware that these inconsistencies and my other human frailties may, indeed, have contributed to my present state. Perhaps, if I had been more vigilant with my self-care, I wouldn't have found myself in that position! On the other hand, since there are no guarantees in life, it was a pointless guessing game to continue that kind of thinking. I didn't want to participate in the "if only" game and be filled with regrets. "IF" was a big word that encouraged doubt and uncertainty. To spend my days feeling regret over what had happened (or what had not) would only create more stress and despair. Without the ability to change the past, I knew focusing on self-doubt was not what I needed. Life had become too precious. Having come through the darkness into the light, I could not give up on myself, nor could I disappoint my Lord and Savior. I was even more convinced He had a plan for my life that I desperately wanted to fulfill.

I believed stress played a major role in my illness. My jobs were always demanding and I was constantly under time constraints. It was common to bring work home on evenings and weekends. I often felt pressure to accomplish one task so I could move to others that awaited. In my work environment, I moved from crisis to crisis. They were never-ending. In my personal life, there wasn't much difference. Again, I moved from one thing to another—most of the time, on a very tight schedule. Every evening was full. So was every weekend. It wasn't unusual to rush into the house, change clothes, and be out the door within minutes, on my way to the next event. Since I was a member of the Stephen Ministry program at church, I made myself available to others who had problems. I always took the time to listen to their concerns. Unfortunately, I did that even when I needed a break, because I believed it was part of my personal ministry. I used physical exercise, walking my dogs, and music as my coping tools. For years, my friends asked, "How can you handle all that stress?" I smiled and replied, "Because I have to. It doesn't usually bother me." *I'm a psych nurse. Of course, I know how to manage stress!* I truly believed I could manage it better than others and actually felt somewhat prideful about my perceived abilities. Sadly, I was deluded.

I was very knowledgeable about how stress takes its toll, but I didn't think about its personal price until I was diagnosed with cancer. The effects of stress can appear long after the stressful moments have passed. I also neglected to remind myself of its cumulative effects, a fact that was particularly applicable to my situation. One of the cancer resources I consulted suggested making a list of the life events that occurred for the 18 months prior to the diagnosis. When I completed this exercise, it became evident a common theme during those months was CHANGE! My friends, job, church, home, support system, and physical move all had changed within that time period. Of course, with these changes came additional stress. This was on top of an already high level of stress I had experienced in Michigan. On a standard stress evaluation scale, I ranked near the top. Stress was something with which I had to contend daily and it became quite clear I was not as good at managing it as I originally thought. Another exercise suggested looking at the benefits I gained from having cancer. As much as I hated to admit, cancer gave me attention, recognition, companionship, and friendships to ease my lonely feelings. It was not a pretty picture and I was appalled with my analysis. *Apparently, I am more needy and self-centered than I ever thought!* Then I realized I needed to find healthy ways of achieving the same outcomes.

In the psychiatric setting, we emphasize you cannot solve a problem until you know what it is. It sounds simple enough, but it really isn't an easy task. The root cause is sometimes very difficult to discover. Once identified, it is then necessary to confront the problem and work with it in whatever constructive way is possible, in order to move beyond it. Therapy and support often make the difference in handling the anguish of the process. The same is true for pain. To face the pain is to walk toward it, to live with it, and to allow oneself to feel every aspect of the hurt that accompanies it. Emotional and physical pain are very real and both are extremely uncomfortable. Denial may work for a while, but it is not successful long term. Pretending the pain doesn't exist only makes it hurt worse and sometimes actually prolongs its effects. So, as difficult as it is, to face the pain head-on is the only action to take for resolution.

From my view, the difficulty with this approach is not knowing how long the pain will continue. We have a tendency to avoid it and will generally choose the approaches that allow us such an option, if they exist. Even if we know our pain may be time-limited (that is, if it will last for a few days, weeks, or months), it can still be very hard to handle while in the midst of it. The most obvious example is the death of a loved one. Most of us know the grieving process takes the better part of a year before one feels somewhat adjusted to the absence of the loved one. However, living through the year can be very rough. In some situations, it may take even longer than a year. When my father died, I was depressed and felt the loss so acutely that I cannot remember what I did for seven months! Even though it included a holiday period (Thanksgiving, Christmas, and New Year, which are my favorite times of the year), I have absolutely no recollection of anything that happened during those months. I obviously went through the daily motions and functioned on some level, but I remember nothing. Had this behavior moved into a period of years, my entire life would have been disrupted. Even when help is available from a trained therapist or family member/friend, there is nothing easy about confronting pain.

My mother always said, "It isn't what happens to you in life, but how you react to it that counts." I believe she was a very wise woman who may have discovered the real secret to our spiritual growth. She confirmed my belief that each of us is in control of our own reactions and emotions. It may the one thing we CAN totally control in our lives.

Someone else doesn't cause us to be angry. Rather, we give ourselves permission to feel the anger because that is the way we have chosen to react. Both my parents taught me to do my personal best every time I took on a task, whether large or small. And yet, they emphasized, when a mistake was made, I should learn from my error. That way, I can change my behavior and avoid repeating the same mistake.

It was from this philosophy that I developed the approach of viewing life events as lessons. *What am I supposed to learn from this experience? What do I need to know? What is this situation revealing about myself?* It is not an easy process to put myself through and sometimes the answers are revealed more easily than other times. Some of the lessons are about a negative aspect of myself, which requires changing. Those are the most painful.

In the last twenty years, I added another element: *What is God trying to tell me?* I felt this question was necessary because I believed God may be trying to answer one of my prayers or help me discern His will for my life. My recurring frustrations are that He doesn't always work at the speed I like or in the particular manner I prefer. But He is at work, which is important to note. I believe when there is an obstacle in life, it is there for a reason.

Furthermore, I believe each of us is dealt the lesson(s) we need to learn! I don't always understand its (or their) significance at the moment, but the message may become clearer at a future point. However, not all of my questions are always answered, and there are times when I may never know the answer while I'm on this earth.

I put obstacles—adversity, pain, and brokenness—in the same category because they are moments of truth that place me in the midst of great personal anguish. Even though I may suffer, God has a way of letting me know He is there. I also think He watches closely to see how I will react to my "obstacles" and then decides how He will use me for His purpose. We usually ask, "Why me, God?" However, perhaps the more appropriate question to ask is "What would you have me do for you, Lord?" This is an example of choosing to live by faith.

To some degree, our obstacles are tests of faith only because we make them so. I don't believe God needs to test us. He has no reason; He loves us completely, as we are. He doesn't love us because of who we are, but because of who He is. God is love. Yet, we often assign a spiritual meaning to the events that occur and place them squarely on His shoulders, as if He chose to drop a challenge upon us. I am convinced that we allow our circumstances to come between us and God, but shouldn't it be the other way around? He stands between us and our circumstances! Certainly, some people have lost their faith in God as a result of some crisis in their life. They felt God caused the problem and so they drew away, feeling disillusioned. Yet, others have become stronger in their faith as a result of the crisis (or crises) they encountered. What has made the difference between the two? In my situations, I believe it was whether I turned toward God or away from Him with my crisis. I think the lesson to learn with pain and adversity is to turn oneself completely toward Him. Lean on Him! That is the true test of faith—to trust in Him when we think we cannot!

Through my brokenness, I discovered what God wanted me to know about Him! He gave me the opportunity to learn this lesson in many ways, which really is the whole theme of this book.

Once I was able to give up my preoccupation with "self" (that is, who is in control) and to become still in His presence, I opened myself wholly to Him. I communicated to Him that I was willing to receive and accept what He has to give. Then He quietly came into my heart! That is when the miracles began to happen.

This was not an easy process for me because, first, I had to admit my own weaknesses. Then I had to turn them over to Him (i.e., truly give them up) and trust in my heart He would take care of me. When I accepted this, it seemed God was at my side instantly, although the truth is He was always there, ready and waiting. I just didn't realize it. However, during my walk in the "valley of darkness," which refers to the period where I was in the midst of my suffering and pain, I realized He wanted me to lean on Him exclusively. This level of trust led to an exquisite opportunity to deepen and strengthen our relationship. It was a win-win relationship. My Lord was pleased; I felt contentment and happiness, both personally and spiritually; and peace and tranquility entered my life on a daily basis! I liked the way Max Lucado said in his book, *God Came Near,* "The next time you find yourself alone in a dark alley facing the undeniables of life, don't cover them with a blanket, or ignore them with a nervous grin. Don't turn up the TV and pretend they aren't there. Instead, stand still, whisper His name, and listen. He is nearer than you think."

I saw my brokenness as an opportunity for God, which became my ultimate blessing. It was there for the purpose of creating growth. God had something in mind for me to accomplish and the experience of pain was necessary. A greater purpose existed than what I could see with my human eyes. He knew my needs and was there to satisfy them. Maybe that is why "Faith is blind" is said. Trusting in Him is so hard to do! Believing something wonderful will emerge from the adversity and that it is for the glory of God is really putting blind faith into action! That is when the pain actually becomes a precious gift. It reminds me of the line, "When you are up to your neck in alligators, it is hard to remember your job was to drain the swamp." How true!

One of the most difficult things to do is to ask God for help and then wait. The waiting often feels like it goes on forever. That is when I may be too quick to give up on Him because I am not getting my answer within the timeframe I expect. Sometimes, I even doubt God heard me in the first place! Over the years, I have been learning about the lesson of patience. It truly is a virtue! I am still trying to develop that fruit of the spirit. God works at His own pace and in His own way—all for a reason. His ways are mysterious and unpredictable and He always delivers a holy surprise. There is nothing I can do to change Him and it would be foolish to try. However, at times, this has led to feelings of abandonment because I erroneously believe He has left me alone to deal with the adverse situation. Honestly, I know this isn't true, but feelings and rational thinking don't travel together, as I have said before.

I have come to realize He is with me in everything I do. It makes no difference in the size or importance of the task because whatever I do should be a reflection of Him and display His glory.

There is a Christian poster which says, "Great occasions for serving God seldom come, but little ones surround us daily." It seems like we are always looking for the big opportunity. As a result, we miss those answers to our prayers which are easily within our reach or the ones standing directly in front of us. Some prayers also take longer to answer, so waiting is required.

When I was in the midst of my pain, waiting was hard to accept and even more difficult to live through!

Adversity forced me to take stock of who I was.

I looked inward to what made up my true self. I had to identify everything and be totally honest about what I saw. It was a distinct challenge to see myself as I truly was—not for the impression I gave to the outside world.

Sometimes, we have been so effective with hiding ourselves that we are confused as to our authentic self. Sifting through the "garbage" and discarding what is no longer needed is a cumbersome process and produces emotional pain of its own!

I kept questioning why I was unable to handle my surgery and chemo by myself. I'm not completely sure why this bothered me so much, but I suspect it related to my pride of being fiercely independent.

With my cancer, I definitely needed the support and assistance of others, which was a very humbling experience. Then I learned the secret: God didn't expect me to go it alone. He was by my side throughout my ordeal.

He also gave me the tools I needed for coping. This came in the form of people, prayers, support, dreams, books, writings, music, etc. He truly promised He would provide, and He did. He used my adverse situation to drive home the point that it is okay to depend on others. It is not a sign of weakness or a flaw in my personality. What it does reflect is my human condition! God knows what I do best and where I can have the most influence in His kingdom.

I am totally convinced He will pick me to fulfill His special purpose when the time is right. There is much I am yet to accomplish in His name and for His glory!

When we encounter brokenness, God mends us and makes us whole. It was exciting to learn that! Beth Moore, founder of Living Proof Ministries, describes it this way: "Every time we've been broken and then allowed God to repair us, the mending becomes part of our equipping." God took my experience of brokenness and repurposed it, and I am now powerfully equipped to share my testimony as a witness to His glory.

During my chemo, I became acutely aware of Jesus' ability to feel my hurt and pain in tandem with me. This was a concept which always escaped my understanding. *If Jesus can feel the pain, why doesn't He just take it away? What is so good with Him having empathy? I want Him to remove it!*

However, we don't grow without adversity. It was the story of Lazarus' death which changed my awareness. While spending time in devotions, the Lord kept directing me to the scriptures about Lazarus and his sisters. I believe I was supposed to understand how much God hurts when we are hurting. The words "Jesus wept" jumped out at me one day, and I suddenly realized how deeply Jesus grieved for the loss of his friend, Lazarus. Similarly, God knew what was going to happen and why it was necessary for Jesus to be on that cross, but

I am sure He still hurt and grieved for His son. He felt Jesus' pain and knew His sacrifice was worth the pain! I am assured God used the dark moments in my life in a similar way. In the midst of my brokenness, He demonstrated His presence for me, too. I knew the tears I cried were also His.

Once I moved to Kentucky, the pace of my life drastically slowed. Initially, since I had not yet made new friends or found a new church, my time was truly my own. I also hadn't acquired any professional commitments that demanded my time, so I could choose what to do. There were days I could do nothing!

That was clearly something I had not experienced since grade school. I embraced the lifestyle change and spent more time with my favorite pastimes like gardening, decorating, and reading. As a result, it was easier to take a more objective view on my life, both personally and professionally.

Most of all, my stress level was much less than it was in Michigan and I felt calmer and happier.

My Spiritual Lesson:

Could I have been convinced there would be greater joy and serenity in my life after being diagnosed with cancer, or that there is a blessing with each lesson we learn in life, or that pain can actually be a gift? The answer is no. Even today, I am shocked when I hear myself say it, but I now know it to be true. There is no doubt He got my attention through my cancer and is moving me forward in His plan. Now I can genuinely thank and praise Him for the opportunity to see life from a new perspective—His! With each life event that occurred, I found myself one step closer to fulfilling His marvelous plan. When I look back, I see God's hand clearly at work. It is amazingly beautiful and I am so thankful for Him!

When I moved to Kentucky, I thought a significant event would occur. That was exactly what happened. The event just turned out to be spiritual in nature. I can't think of anything more exciting! Yes, the pain was necessary. He didn't cause it to happen, but He did use it to His benefit—and to mine. What is the message from this? The Lord showed me the depth of His love, and I also learned His mercy is on the other side of brokenness. What an incredible blessing!

"Be thankful in all circumstances. This is what God wants from you in your life in union with Christ Jesus." (I Thessalonians 5:18, Good News Study Bible)

THE 9th SIGN: A LITTLE MORE PEPPER

"Trust in the Lord with all your heart and lean not on your own understanding; in all your ways submit to Him, and He will make your paths straight. Do not be wise in your own eyes; fear the Lord and shun evil. This will bring health to your body and nourishment to your bones." (Proverbs 3:5-8, NIV)

Before I started chemo, I had beautiful auburn hair. I loved the color and it suited me well. My friends called me the "outrageous redhead" and I enjoyed the nickname. I believed the red hair gave me permission to do and say whatever I wanted because people expected it from a redhead. With my wild and crazy sense of humor, I usually took advantage of most situations and was quick to credit it to the color of my hair. I was not a natural redhead although I had strong red highlights and was very fair-skinned and freckled. My brother had natural red hair but a darker complexion. It was like our hair and complexions were backwards. I used to joke how God doesn't usually make mistakes, but He sure did on this one! If I could have had one wish granted, it would have been for red hair. It was that important!

Since I had been told my hair would fall out following the second treatment, I decided to be proactive and purchase a wig. My hairdresser, Shelia, volunteered to help and I was grateful for her offer. We arranged a day for shopping and planned to visit the one wig shop in town. If nothing could be found, she was willing to travel to a nearby city. She wanted me to be satisfied.

I dreaded this shopping excursion because I had a strange sense of foreboding. I attributed it to feeling stressed over my cancer diagnosis. I figured it was just my own anxiety creating doubt.

Upon entering the wig shop, I noticed a woman sitting behind a desk, holding a baby. A young woman was seated in front of her. I assumed it was the owner, her daughter, and grandchild. They were very preoccupied with one another and engaged in their conversation.

I then looked around and saw shelves lined with multiple wigs. Instantly, I felt overwhelmed. I hesitated.

Then the lady called out, "Are you here to buy a wig?"

It was a stupid comment and it irritated me. *Lady, really? Why else would I be here?*

Next, she yelled out, "Is this for fun or do you have cancer?"

I was finished.

I turned to Shelia and said, "Let's get out of here! I don't want to stay."

Shelia tried to calm me while telling the store owner our trip wasn't for fun. I felt a mixture of panic and anger rising to the surface and I wanted to leave immediately.

"Shelia, I can't stay here. I can't do this. I am going." I blurted this out while walking toward the door. I was embarrassed at the insensitivity of this woman and wanted no part of her.

Shelia intervened by begging me to sit down while she began looking for a wig. I complied.

We both ignored the lady and focused on our task. The lady continued her conversation with her daughter and never offered any assistance. Shelia quickly found a wig similar to my hairstyle. With a little trimming, she said it would be perfect. When I learned it was on sale, it helped me feel better. Shelia paid for it and we left.

I had no further interactions with the shop owner as she was content to focus her time and energy on her grandchild. I felt she was rude. Honestly, I didn't want to purchase anything there, but I didn't want to go elsewhere, either. I already felt vulnerable and victimized by having cancer, and this experience compounded those feelings! In the past, I would have spoken up and told her how I felt. However, this time, I just couldn't do it. A year later, I wrote a letter to the shop owners that shared my feelings from my shopping experience. I hoped her eyes would be opened by reading my comments. Unfortunately, I never received any kind of reply, nor did I enter her shop again. I have no idea if she learned a lesson.

There were no words to describe the feelings I experienced when my hair began to fall out. The word "traumatic" doesn't even come close! My friend, Kim, told me what to expect, but it was still terrifying! I cried as I stood in the shower and watched the hair gather around my feet on the tile floor. The more water touched it, the more it fell out. When I left the shower and was getting dressed, it continued to come out with the least provocation. If I touched it ever so lightly, it fell out in huge clumps. I became fearful to comb it, because I was sure I would have nothing left. Blowing it dry added too much stress to it, so I let it dry naturally. This became my coping pattern. I tried not to stress my hair in any manner. Even if there was the slightest breeze, my hair would fall out. Every morning, I awakened to find a pile of hair on the pillow. The only way to collect and remove it was to run a comb over the pillow. It made me sick to my stomach. There seemed to be hair everywhere, except on my head. I hated it! I felt naked and was certain I had become bald in one day! The truth was I never did lose all my hair. Perhaps it was mere stubbornness on my part or I willed it not to happen. Maybe it was because I was so angry with the doctor for telling me it was a certainty. Who knows? I never once wore the wig! My hair became quite thin, especially at the crown, but I didn't cover my head. I knew I looked like a cancer patient, but I didn't want to wear a scarf or hat to advertise my status. Instead, I viewed my thin hair as my "badge of courage" to the world. It was a constant reminder of the cross I was bearing.

After chemo was completed, the wig sat on a dresser in my spare room. It came to represent all that was rotten and miserable about my experience. All my anguish must have been displaced onto the wig because it was surrounded with a veil of darkness. The store owner's reaction and my anger resulting from the shopping experience were the final straws. I'm sure they added to my hatred of that wig. I considered setting the wig afire and taking pleasure watching it be destroyed. I thought that act would symbolically represent my rebirth, like a phoenix rising from the ashes! For a while, I regretted wasting my money on the purchase, but I soon realized it served a useful purpose. In some small way, it helped me regain a sense of control over a traumatic life experience!

Harder to handle than the thinning of the hair was its color change. As soon as my hair began falling out, its color went from red to white—within six weeks! For a while, I had white hair with red tips. It was truly ugly, but what was I to do? I tried to make light of it, but I really hated it. The CEO of the hospital commented on my hair color one day. To put him at ease, I mentioned I was starting a new trend in Kentucky. I was asking all of my friends and associates to "tip" their hair similar to mine since it was a popular style in California. I thought this action would represent others' empathy. He asked how many people had I convinced?

I said, "None!" We both laughed.

"Will your hair grow back in the red color?"

"No," I replied.

"Why not?"

I told him I had been coloring my hair for years, but now my roots were white. He blushed and it was obvious he didn't realize red was not my original color.

Many people at work told me they liked the mainly white mixture I had, but I thought they were lying to make me feel better. From my perspective, the white hair removed all color from my face and made me look old and ugly. Most of all, I felt obsolete!

Before I had completed the chemo series, my hair began to grow back. It started about a month before my last treatment. I didn't connect the dots because I was still receiving the same drugs, so it didn't make sense why my hair would suddenly be growing again. One morning, I noticed a brown shadow at the hairline on the top of my head. *What is this?* So many problems had emerged during the course of my treatment that I looked at this issue as another one.

Upon examination, I realized the brown color was new hair growth! Then the brown began to appear on the sides and, finally, all over the head. Honestly, it looked bizarre! I thought the white color might change to brown, but then I saw white fuzzy hairs on my head, too. I had no idea what the final color would be!

Within a month following the last treatment, my hair became decidedly thicker. I could no longer see my scalp through my hair. It was interesting that its texture also changed. This gave me a sense of relief because, while I was in the midst of chemo, my hair would literally disintegrate when touched. Now, it felt like hair!

In the two weeks before Christmas, my hair grew over an inch! It was also so thick that it was impossible to get a comb or brush through it. Both my hairdresser and I were astonished! Shelia kept noticing the changes when I got a haircut, which was every two weeks. I wanted to keep my hair in a short style, so frequent haircuts were necessary.

For a while, it looked like my hair would be straight, but the natural curls and waves returned. My hair had become a mixture of brown, gray, and mostly white. Although this new mixture was not my favorite, I decided not to color it again. One male co-worker referred to it as "salt and pepper that could use a little more pepper!" I thought his comment was cute and it really helped me accept the color. It also confirmed my previous decision to go *au naturel*. I had entered a new phase of life and desired being more loving and accepting of myself. It was important to see me as God sees me.

The only side effect of the chemo for which I was thankful was the loss of hair on my legs. Since shaving every other day was my normal routine, I was delighted to shave my legs only once a month during my treatments. Even when the hair returned, it was baby fine and almost invisible. I was ecstatic!

My reprieve was short-lived, however. After the chemo was finished, the hair returned on my legs in its former state—thick and dark!

My Spiritual Lesson:

There were actually many lessons I learned from God during my "hair-raising" (or hair-losing) experience—not just one!

Strange as it may sound, the first one was the actual loss of hair, because it verified the chemo was working! God was clearly demonstrating that healing was taking place in my body. The fast-growing cancer cells were being destroyed along with the fast-growing hair follicles. This was our goal! All was good!

The second lesson was more challenging. It was the task of learning how to accept and love myself as I was and to stop being so critical of how I looked. Without a doubt, to adjust to the thinning hair and its changing colors was a major accomplishment. It was something I never thought possible. I began viewing my hair color as a special symbol of God's love. Although there were some brown hairs, the primary color was white. Even so, there were some hairs around my temple that were even whiter. The effect was a highlight that accentuated my face. I considered it a gift from God. With a paintbrush in hand, He dipped into the white paint and casually streaked the hair around my face. It gave me a special glow. A friend who had not seen me since the change was speechless when I saw him. He commented how much he liked it and thought I paid "big bucks" to achieve the look. Laughingly, I told him he was right. I had paid a significant price, but not in the way he thought. I accepted the fact that God's light shone through me and I was marked in a loving way by Him. My hair became a constant reminder to radiate His love through my witness to others.

The third lesson related to the issue of trust. I realized there were plenty of circumstances and events in life that I could not control, but the one thing I do have control over is that of trusting God. I will be cared for completely if I rely on Him. There would be no need for anxiety and worry. I believed He was urging me to change this aspect of myself, once and for all.

Finally, I recognized He allowed the wig to become the focal point for my anger and rage—of which there was plenty. Without such a symbol, I could have turned the anger inward, where it would have festered and, ultimately, damaged my ability to move toward health and healing. Or I could have directed anger toward God permanently and hated Him for making me go through this experience. That approach would not have yielded a good outcome, either. Instead, I was able to experience God's great love, concern, and care regardless of what my circumstance was.

"God is our refuge and strength, an ever-present help in trouble." (Psalm 46:1, NIV)

RITA CARBUHN

THE 10th SIGN: THIS MOMENT IN TIME

"Yes, my soul, find rest in God; my hope comes from Him. Truly, He alone is my rock and my salvation; He is my fortress. I will not be shaken. My salvation and my honor depend on God, He is my might rock, my refuge. Trust in him at all times, you people; pour out your hearts to Him, for God is our refuge." (Psalm 62:5-8, NIV)

I made vacation plans with my friend, Bonnie, in February, before my diagnosis of cancer. We decided to travel to North Carolina in September.

Our plan was to meet in Norfolk, rent a car, and drive to the Outer Banks for a week of sun and fun. Tickets were purchased in May, before my surgery, and I expected to be fully recovered by fall. It seemed like the perfect plan for complete relaxation. Both of us needed time to unwind.

Then chemo entered the picture!

As the months passed and the side effects from my chemo increased, I became less sure I could follow through with our plan. Bonnie and I talked weekly, trying to decide what made sense.

The decision was mine because I was the best judge of whether I could handle the trip—physically and emotionally. I consulted my oncologist.

"Go," he said. "The break will be beneficial to you."

I agreed.

Actually, I believed it was absolutely essential, because I was at the end of my rope and wanted to give up. I desperately needed a respite.

In August, I realized the trip fell between treatments. No special arrangements would have to be made, nor would any treatments be delayed. It seemed as though the trip was meant to be! I then believed my remaining months might be easier with a break. Realizing how all this was playing out made me more excited! Even a hurricane that hit the area in the week before our departure didn't deter us. We knew if there was too much damage to follow through with our original plan, we would develop an alternate one. What was most important was having time to renew our souls! Nothing was going to stop us!

Bonnie was scheduled to arrive in Norfolk an hour earlier, so I told her to look for a white-haired woman instead of a redhead. I believed she needed a warning so she wouldn't be shocked, but I could tell she still was startled when we met. She even admitted as much. However, within a short time, she grew accustomed to my new look. She even managed to put me at ease with my appearance, too. I had a wonderful week. I suffered no nausea nor an upset stomach, so I could eat what I wanted. I even had a couple of drinks, which had no ill effects. I didn't have much energy but there isn't a lot required when vacationing at the beach.

We walked on the beach at least twice daily, picked up shells, and soaked up the warm rays of the sun. When we were sunning each day, I napped often and caught up on sleep. Whenever we were feeling too hot, we slipped into the ocean for a quick dip to cool down. This routine was repeated multiple times each day. I even tanned to a golden brown, which was a first! I had been warned to be careful with the sun which, I assumed, meant I would burn more easily. The cycle of burning and peeling was always my pattern, so I planned for the possibility of severe sunburn. To protect myself, I purchased extra sunscreen, hats, and beach cover-ups.

Despite the fact I slathered myself with these lotions, my body tanned to a deeper brown every time I was in the sun. Bonnie commented she had never known me to have a tan. I was as shocked as she was, especially when I looked in the mirror! *Who is this white-haired, tanned woman I see in the reflection?* When I was in the shower, my brown legs seemed even browner against the white of the shower walls. I kept thinking someone else had joined me because those certainly couldn't be MY legs! I had to laugh at the newness of my brown body, but I grew accustomed to it. I never burned or peeled once during the week! The only problem I encountered was conjunctivitis and a runny nose. No one else on the beach carried a box of tissues like I did!

Yet, there was a minor problem to which I had to adjust. Whenever I wore my bathing suit, I was aware my surgical scars from the portacath insertion were very noticeable. At first, it seemed like everyone we passed on our beach walks looked at the bright red scars on my chest rather than looking my face. The scars were very obvious and I felt self-conscious about them. So, I wore a cover-up for the first couple of days. After that, I decided these scars were mine to claim and I altered my attitude.

Why should I care what others think? These are part of my identity and I should not feel embarrassed! The cover-up was discarded the rest of the trip!

The Atlantic Ocean, the Outer Banks, and the warm September days were very soothing and healing. Time stopped and I basked in the "moments." The sound of the waves lapping against the shore in their rhythmical pattern calmed me to the core of my being. I envisioned myself as one with the ocean and its surroundings. I flew with the seagulls over the sea and dipped into the water to get my meal along with them. I ran on the beach with the little sandpipers as they darted back and forth to avoid the water on the shore. I was the mighty wave rushing up on the shore with such great force and then flowing back to the sea in its own squiggly pattern.

During the day, with the sun high in the sky, I was one with the sun. I felt its reds and oranges on my closed eyelids as I lay on the sand and melted in the goodness of its warmth. I entered a state of mindlessness and couldn't bring myself to do anything other than exist for the moment. I soaked up all of life and pulled as much as I could manage into my being. I was totally in tune with my surroundings, in every way possible. My senses were keener than they had ever been. Colors were more vibrant and alive! The smell of the sea would awaken me from a deep sleep and bring me back to the reality of where I was. The birds talked to me through their chirps and screeches and I felt we were communicating in a manner that had never before been possible. I became aware when we were entering their space. They squawked at us when we were disturbing them and would scurry out of our way as we came near. On other days, they seemed to follow us, cocking their heads and looking at us in mysterious ways—almost as if they were listening to our conversation as we walked on the beach.

The endless horizon and smoothness of the ocean in the distance nearly lulled me into believing I could walk on the water and follow a path into oblivion. The beach sand smoothed the calluses on my feet. I took pleasure in feeling the different textures of the sand—from the soft, gritty sand near the bank to the cool, hard sand next to the shore. It was all wonderfully relaxing on the feet! At times, the peace surrounding us would be disturbed by a sudden gust of wind that caused sand to fly everywhere. It got into our eyes, hair, bathing suits, and beach bags. If the wind was too strong, sand splattered against us like a million tiny needles pricking our bodies. On those days, we left early. In the evenings, we would walk again on the beach and soak up the ever-changing—and yet unchanging—world around us.

Eventually, the blackness of the night descended, but it didn't alter our pattern.

Once the darkness arrived, the stars beckoned us to jump into the sky to join them. It felt as though we could reach out and touch them because they were so near. Floating in the air toward them seemed as possible as breathing.

Lounging in the deck chairs at night, wearing a sweatshirt to keep warm, I felt the world had stopped. Nothing existed except the sound and smell of the sea, the black of the night, the gleam of the stars, and the feel of the wind against our faces. Talking to each other was unnecessary, as it only disrupted the peacefulness and tranquility of the moment. The beauty was just overwhelming!

"Sameness" reigned supreme and yet nothing was truly the same. The constancy of life revealed itself daily, but there were also surprises, in every direction I looked.

Each morning, I watched the sunrises and marveled at the changing colors in the sky. Once the sun came over the horizon, the line of the sunlight on the water raced toward me and then reached up on the shore to grab my legs and pull me near. I was mesmerized by the timelessness of the moment and the dependable pattern of the earth's cycles.

Sunsets were equally as enthralling. We stood on the tallest of sand dunes and watched the sun disappear behind the horizon, leaving an endless array of pinks, oranges, purples, reds, and yellows to ooh and aah over. Then, ever so quickly, the sky would become so dark that we hurried to find our way off the huge dune before the blackness engulfed us and we were lost.

Although I tried to capture these sights on film, I knew my photographs wouldn't portray the mood as I experienced it in real life. So, I was challenged to imprint the scenic and mesmerizing pictures deep within the inner recesses of my mind. In this way, I hoped to be able to call the memories forward on a future day when I needed an escape from the world!

Life was never as real as it was that week. It existed in every second of time. It was precious and I was part of it! Max Lucado, a Christian minister and author, describes such a moment as an "eternal instant," defined as "an instant in time that had no time—a moment that was lifted off the timeline and amplified into a forever so all the angels could witness its majesty."

My vacation week was clearly one of those moments! I was enormously appreciative of what God had created and thankful He was allowing me to be alive to enjoy it. I tried to take in every experience as though it was my last one on earth. I knew there was nothing better than this moment in time! I couldn't even fathom how heaven could surpass what God provided us on earth!

I didn't talk about cancer and the chemo unless I was asked. For most of the week, it just didn't exist either in my mind or in my life.

All that changed when we arrived on Ocracoke Island.

During the 2½ days we spent there, we met a very delightful couple from Virginia. Maybe it was because our rooms were adjacent to one another or because we found ourselves sitting together on the deck every evening, but we were drawn toward each other.

In our many talks, we learned that Bonnie and Dick had mutual acquaintances and had actually grown up in the same schools, only a few years apart. Polly had experienced both the loss of her father and mother during that year, so we shared her grief. Then we talked about other changes we experience as we grow older.

They supported me as I told my story about breast cancer and my ongoing struggles with the chemo. We tried to make sense of our lives as we dined on fresh salmon pâté, wheat crackers, and beer or wine.

Most of all, we talked and laughed and were there for each other as we shared both happy and sad memories. In that short period of time, a friendship was born.

When it came time to say goodbye, we felt as though we were losing special friends. We exchanged addresses and phone numbers and vowed to keep in touch. We even talked about getting together the following year for a reunion. Bonnie and I were touched by the closeness. We knew we were chosen recipients of an unusual and wonderful gift, but we didn't know why. Nonetheless, we were thankful.

Little did I realize this story was not to end here!

I thought the respite would renew my spirits and supply the strength, both physically and mentally, to breeze through the remaining treatments. I anticipated an easier time when I returned, but I was wrong. Perhaps, in some ways, it was even harder because I had a taste of an exhilarating stress-free week, which was precious beyond words! I wanted that feeling back! I also desired it on a more permanent basis.

My memory reverted to when I had taken so many things for granted. I longed to return to those magical days when life was good. It was a time I didn't fully appreciate. I didn't want to think about my struggles anymore.

After I returned from my vacation, I wanted to figure out a way to recapture the feelings I experienced during that week. I wanted to live them every day and was sure there had to be a way, but I was at a loss to figure out how!

My Spiritual Lesson:

Hindsight really is a beautiful gift. It's always easier to look back to comprehend the meaning of an event than to try to understand it at the time of its occurrence.

Once I had time to review the wonder of those vacation days, I learned a valuable lesson. I needed to live for each moment and appreciate the "here and now."

All I can affect is today. Tomorrow is as much out of my reach as yesterday is. It doesn't make sense to want something so badly that I overlook what is within my grasp today.

Someone recently told me, "Today is a gift. That is why it is called the present." There is a lot of truth in that statement.

This is actually part of a famous quote by Bil Keane, who said, "Yesterday is history. Tomorrow is a mystery. Today is a gift. That is why it is called the present."

After analyzing my feelings, I vowed to live each day, one at a time. I also wanted to tell people how much I love and appreciate them. The vacation, I'm sure, was a sign that peace and tranquility could be achieved daily, if I would allow myself such a blessing, but also that I needed to spend individual time with God. He was certainly ready. The key was whether I was willing to change my ways and live differently, from that point forward. It was obvious to me that He and I had entered a new dimension with our relationship. Furthermore, I was opening myself to a realm of wonderful possibilities in the days ahead if I allowed His plan to unfold.

THE 11th SIGN: WINDOWS

"Bear one another's burdens, and in this way, you will fulfill the law of Christ." (Galatians 6:2, NRSV)

At a time when I was separated from family and friends, God gave me a burden to carry that I could not handle alone. It was beyond my understanding as to why He would place me in such a situation. I had obeyed His direction to take the job in Kentucky and I thought this meant something wonderful was awaiting. After all, when you were obedient to God's leading, wasn't that supposed to be rewarded?

But instead of good things happening, I was facing the worst time of my life! My move from Michigan had created a split from my existing support system. Plus, with my family living in Arizona and Texas, I truly was alone. I was puzzled why He was asking me to struggle for my very life without support. But I overlooked one major factor—when God closes a door, He opens a window. In my case, these windows were the people who ended up supporting me, especially through my crisis of cancer.

Shortly before the diagnosis of cancer, I discovered my newest friend, Kim. She was a woman who, seven years earlier, was diagnosed with Hodgkin's disease. She suffered through chemotherapy and radiation and managed to come out on the other side as a healthy and whole person. Kim was my major support in all respects from Day One. She cried with me when I needed to shed tears; she gave me hope when I had none; and she offered her strength when I thought I couldn't go on. We laughed and giggled together like little kids when we found things were hysterically funny. When I was angry at the world and hated everything that was happening, she gave me the opportunity to express my feelings and not be judged.

She gave herself daily, which is the greatest gift one can give another as we know from the example of Jesus. Any secrets she discovered in managing cancer were shared. Even her husband, who functioned as her rock during her illness, gave me suggestions on how to cope. I labeled his recommendations as "Ken's tidbits."

Each day, I looked forward to his most recent suggestion. Since Kim and I worked together, I saw her daily. I saw Jesus in her loving actions and was so thankful God was continuing to watch over me through her.

I don't know what I would have done without her support and assistance. What I do know is that God placed her there because He knew my need.

The second major support was my Kentucky minister, Jim. We talked for many hours about the impending surgery and he listened to my fears and concerns. He was present during each of my surgical events, to pray and to help me feel safe and secure in God's arms. I was thankful for his friendship and love. His sense of humor and obvious caring made a difference.

During my recovery, he came to my house and brought my mother and me fresh strawberries from his garden. We talked and laughed for what seemed like hours and his presence was very healing. I know he prayed for me daily, as did many other members in my church. I felt very loved and accepted. I knew God had led me to the church where Jim pastored because that was where I was supposed to be.

Even though I had numerous friends in Michigan, I stopped hearing from them when I moved. I think it was because I was far away and their own lives were busy. Some were occupied with young children and I knew their priorities changed, due to the kids. I could understand having little available time to write or call. All in all, there were about eight people who kept in regular contact. I had figured the ones who were most likely to keep in touch were those in the Chatterstitch group, but that wasn't the case; there appeared to be some truth to the saying, "Out of sight, out of mind."

I could understand this behavior, as I had been guilty of doing it myself. I knew it wasn't something that happened only when you moved to another state. I, too, had allowed some of my friendships to fall by the wayside, even when we lived in the same town! Now, however, I realized how much it hurt to be ignored and forgotten. I was surprised at how very much alone I felt from this lack of contact.

Those who did maintain contact did so in unique ways and they were all very meaningful.

One person was quite methodical in her approach. I heard from her on a weekly basis for eight months. She wrote even when she was on vacation or building and moving into a new home. I received a card before each treatment which she said she was praying on my behalf.

Her messages of love and words of encouragement were very comforting and a great source of strength to me. Her actions exemplified Christianity as its best and I knew she loved and cared as much as Jesus did.

She continued to write to me, until her death several years later. I thought her actions were a beautiful example of unconditional love. To reach out to each other and be there in times of need is one of the generous gifts of love we have to offer others.

There were many other people who wrote frequently, to keep my spirits up. I came to value those letters because I could read them often. This activity kept me going, especially when I didn't feel well. Some friends started calling instead of writing. It was so nice to hear their voices, but the calls were brief. I truly enjoyed our exchanges of conversation even though I did not always feel up to talking for long. I felt I was cheating them because I didn't feel well to talk. Most of them expressed sadness and concern with us being so far apart. They felt helpless, as did I. Some said all they could do was pray—but, from my perspective, that was not a little thing! Just knowing they were praying was quite enough! The words "thank you" never seemed adequate, to express my appreciation.

Many former employees, associates, and other acquaintances sent cards, notes, poems, etc. All were comforting! Even my mother's friends in Arizona asked about me and prayers were shared within her church on my behalf! So many people told me they were lifting me up in prayer that I was literally prayed for in dozens of churches in ten states throughout the country! I felt the power in their prayers because I felt enveloped with God's love. I felt very honored and humbled with such a gift!

Daily, I was asked about my health status by multiple hospital employees. Some were friends, but I knew many others only slightly. I believed I looked like a cancer patient, so I assumed that was their motive for asking. I usually replied with a simple answer and thanked them for their inquiry, but I also wondered what they knew and who had told them. Had my privacy and confidentiality been compromised?

However, I found no evidence of a breach. My friend, Kim, reminded me it was the nature of the "hospital family" in this community. She said they were concerned and were merely expressing their empathy. I accepted her explanation. While at work, I chose not to dwell on my illness or talk about my cancer. I needed a distraction from my misery. Work provided that much-needed diversion. My staff called me the "iron woman" because they believed I was strong, but I had problems accepting their label.

How can they see me as strong? Lord, I don't feel strong. I am weak and miserable! I'm not handling this cancer well at all! They have to be lying to make me feel better! Isn't it interesting how we see ourselves so differently from others' views of us?

"Expect to lose some friends because of your cancer," Kim commented one day. I thought she was crazy! I didn't think it was possible, but she still warned me not to be surprised. And then it happened!

First of all, one very close friend had stopped communicating with me when I moved to Kentucky. I knew she was busy with her job, school, and family, so I overlooked her insensitivity. Although I was hurt, I thought I would hear from her once she learned of my cancer. After all, we were like sisters and had pledged always to be there for each other. Days passed without any word. I knew she was aware of my diagnosis, so her lack of contact honestly confused me.

When I talked with mutual friends, they were unable to explain her behavior. They were just as puzzled. Finally, I decided to take the matter into my own hands. I wrote a letter to share my feelings and to apologize if I had offended her. I asked for an honest reply and wanted her forgiveness if I hurt her. I explained how much I missed our friendship and how pivotal she had been in my life.

Then I waited.

Nine months passed.

The silence continued. It became deafening. It was apparent she had no intention to respond, which saddened me. Finally, in the year after my cancer, I received a card with one brief note: "There are so many problems in our relationship if we chose to resolve them in this lifetime!" *What exactly does this mean? I waited for this? It isn't even grammatically correct and makes no sense!* All I felt was more confusion. It appeared she had no desire to resolve anything and I was left hanging! What I think she was trying to say is she believed there were many problems with our relationship (although I had no idea what she thought they were), and that we couldn't resolve these problems even if we wanted to do so. I could only shake my head in disbelief while anger, resentment, and bitterness swirled inside.

I found myself dwelling on who was right or wrong, but then I quickly realized laying blame was not helpful. I pondered the best way to handle my feelings and prayed for direction. Immediately, an answer emerged. God led me to the song, "A Season in Your Path," by a Christian artist, Wayne Watson. In it he said, "I'm sure God alone deciphers when people need each other most." Well, this was the answer! It was time to let this relationship go. As sad as it was, it was the right thing to do.

My hope was to appreciate both the happy and sad in our relationship. I tried to focus on an "attitude of gratitude" for what we once had. It was a distinct loss, but God helped me resolve those feelings. I never responded to her letter, nor have we ever had any further contact. If she was here, I would use Wayne Watson's word to say, "I'm thankful for a season in your past."

There was a second casualty, although the loss actually began prior to my cancer and I had not seen it coming. Unfortunately, cancer played a role in its demise. There was a man whom I had been dating while in Michigan. Although he supported my move and wanted to continue seeing me, it became apparent our relationship was not working.

When I was at my lowest point during chemo, I found out he stole from me and was simply using me. As soon as I learned of the theft and his manipulation, I kicked him out of my life permanently. All trust was destroyed. He had become detrimental to my health and healing, and I didn't need that stress. God helped the truth to be revealed and rescued me.

Why was it necessary to have any casualties? I don't know, but my friend was right. People grow apart. Other times, we get fooled by what we thought was good. Sometimes people—or the reasons for the friendships—change!

Being a cancer survivor made me more aware of some irrational thinking and behaviors that persist with a cancer diagnosis. A few people were at a loss to know what to say. They felt awkward, uncomfortable, and remained silent. The longer the silence continued, the greater the discomfort, causing our relationship to end.

For others, the threat of losing a friend to death was too overwhelming, so it was easier to avoid me than to deal with the possibility of my death. I didn't expect to understand all the reasons, but I had to accept the reality that some relationships would end. Some cancer patients I talked to shared they had lost friendships because their acquaintances saw themselves more susceptible to cancer through their association with a cancer patient/survivor! I found this misconception to be astonishing!

Those of us who have faced death have learned to live our lives differently. The blissful ignorance of life has disappeared. Priorities changed, as a result, and we don't ever take things for granted again. The unique experiences we have had with our cancer helped us look at life with new eyes. For me, there was a desire to make the "ordinary become the extraordinary" and the "common become the miraculous." It was possible! I have learned to appreciate how important loving others is and telling them how I feel. I have less tolerance for wasting my time on tasks, relationships, and other things that yield little in return. Each moment in my life is viewed as special because it is another day to enjoy the abundance God has provided. All days should be celebrated with joy, praise, and thanksgiving! Isn't this what Jesus tried to teach us?

Cancer can take, but it can also give. The gifts are many, if we only open our eyes to see them. The new relationships that formed because of my cancer were definite reasons to jump for joy! New dimensions in my existing relationships were also revealed. I am certain those came about because I changed—I opened myself to all possibilities and became willing to live with a new level of awareness and a sense of appreciation for the world around me. Joy meant God was truly present in every moment of my life. Most exciting was my relationship with Jesus. I came to know and love Him more intimately. He was my greatest blessing and gift!

As I reviewed the vacation in the Outer Banks, I knew it was unusual that Bonnie and I would feel so close to two people we had just met. Initially, I referred to it as one of those odd events that just happens in our lives. However, God doesn't create coincidences, so I was certain there was a greater purpose. My answer arrived three weeks after I returned from vacation. One evening, Polly called. She was checking on my status, but also wanted to reveal she had been diagnosed with breast cancer. She discovered a lump while on Ocracoke Island, but chose not to say anything until she saw her doctor. Her lump was cancerous and she was trying to determine what to do. Surgery was being considered, but they had recommended a course of chemo and radiation first.

We talked at length about her situation. I was saddened with her news, but also realized God had brought us together for such a time as this.

Our meeting was a divine appointment. God had designated me to be her support! I needed to pay it forward.

Many months later, a friend told me, "If you believe in coincidences, you probably aren't a strong Christian." At first, I thought this statement was rather radical and then I remembered this incident and the many other similar events I have encountered in my life. There is truth in this statement. God does work in mysterious ways! Sadly, Polly's cancer was more advanced and her treatment was not successful. She died within the year!

In addition to bonding with Polly, I discovered other exquisite treasures within my existing relationships. An example of this was found in a letter I received from one of my male Christian friends during the holidays. Much to my surprise, I learned that man had battled cancer as a teen! I never knew his story. He was (and still is) a very healthy individual. It proves the point we can't make assumptions about another person's life simply by meeting them, which is something we tend to do. His good outcome, he believed, was due to his determination and positive attitude. He also saw his cancer as a temporary hurdle to overcome so he could fulfill all the promises God had in store for him.

His message was one of hope, faith, and encouragement.

He wrote, "We have within ourselves the capacity to 'move mountains' with our faith and will. Let your inner spirit be your guide and trust in the power and love of God."

I was encouraged with his words and was in tears by the time I finished reading his letter. I thought it was awesome that he took the time to share his wisdom. He certainly learned life is a sacred gift!

I also uncovered aspects within the relationships I had at work, of which I was previously unaware.

One of my male co-workers became one of my best supports, despite the fact that he was 15 years younger. He was the Housekeeping Supervisor in the hospital. Since our paths crossed frequently, we developed a close relationship.

On the day I received my diagnosis, he happened to be outside my office and heard me crying. He knocked on the door and came into my office to offer support. He verbally comforted me when I cried and expressed his sadness at the news. Then, in a manner only he could manage, he called me a "tough old bird" and said he knew I would flourish with this diagnosis. I smiled because it was so typical of his zany sense of humor. He appeared aloof and rather gruff on the exterior but, underneath, was warm and caring.
From that point forward, he left a piece of candy and a note of encouragement on my desk almost every day! He frequently

stopped by my office on his rounds or joined me at lunch. Often, I didn't feel well, but he was comfortable with just sitting quietly with me, even when I didn't want to talk. He always tried to lift my spirits and it worked. By the end of our time together, I usually managed a smile.

On another day, a different co-worker sent me a note saying how much he admired my "deep commitment... toward your faith and comrades." He continued, "The strength that you show through your adversities is softened by the sensitivities you have toward others." These little acts of caring often carried me through some of my more difficult and challenging days.

My boss took the news of my cancer amazingly well and wouldn't consider any outcome other than a positive one. He allowed me to work at home on the days I was feeling so ill that I couldn't function adequately. I didn't abuse his generous gift.

All my treatments were scheduled for Fridays so I could have the weekend to recover. This plan worked well until the last couple of months, when I needed an additional day or two. On the days I felt good, I made up time by working evenings. My staff were excellent in handling their tasks and many of my peers assisted if there was a problem and I was unavailable. I couldn't have asked for more cooperation. What was most meaningful was the level of understanding and support that my boss provided. His attitude was an essential factor in my recovery. I certainly couldn't have progressed as well without his acceptance.

Another impactful moment was when I revealed my cancer diagnosis and upcoming surgery to the hospital's CEO.

I felt terribly guilty because I had just returned from a previous surgical event (the hysterectomy) that caused me to be off work for seven weeks. Then I received this news and expected to be off six more weeks. I felt like a loser. The facility had hired me from out of state and all I had done since joining the staff was take time for surgery. I had never been seriously ill in any job where I required extended time off. Here, it appeared I was moving from one surgical event to the next. When I mentioned that to the CEO, he was very understanding. He told me not to worry because they would cover my pay and time off. He suggested I concentrate on taking care of myself because that was more important! Then he offered to pray! He also shared that his sister-in-law had breast cancer and successfully navigated the treatment. He said she was doing well and he saw no reason why I couldn't do the same. It was so apparent God was continuing to bless me!

The number of cards and letters I received was almost overwhelming, but I loved every one. They contained tender and loving affirmations, as well as words of hope, faith, and encouragement. All were powerful and moved me to tears. I had friends who wished they could take away my pain. Others told me how precious I was to them and how much they loved and missed me. Still others wrote words of support and faith such as "Hang in there," "You can do it," "I'm with you," "You are a strong and courageous lady," "God loves you and so do we," and "God will assure you of good health." I didn't feel I measured up to their impressions, but their points of light encouraged me to continue moving forward. Even my former boyfriend's parents sent a letter which touched me deeply. They called my Christmas letter "inspirational" and said my healing was the best gift they received that year. The love they expressed was a beautiful blessing in return!

Friends, neighbors, and acquaintances gave generously of their time and assistance. I was accompanied to the chemo treatments by many people, each of whom was willing to sit and pray while my treatment was in progress. Others brought meals or flowers. I was given baskets of various goodies and supplied with books, tapes, and music. One person mowed my lawn throughout the summer and refused to take any payment. I was thankful for the help because I didn't have the energy to cut the grass myself. Some people stayed with me on the weekend following my treatments, just to make sure I was okay. My trash was often taken to the curb and the container replaced by my neighbors. Hanging plants on my front porch were watered and fertilized. The sidewalk and driveway were edged on a regular basis. Even two trees were planted by a co-worker and her husband! Another couple planted new roses and mulched them while another neighbor fertilized mine when she did hers.

These acts were loving gifts and I thanked God for every one of them. I was so blessed!

My Spiritual Lesson:

Friends bring both joy and pain. Sometimes, the feelings co-exist simultaneously. At other times, they come in waves of one or the other. I experienced both during the year. In the book, *How to Handle Adversity*, Charles Stanley wrote, "The ultimate measure of friends is not where they stand in times of comfort and convenience, but where they stand in times of challenge and controversy."

I learned this lesson painfully. I learned love is like a rare and precious gem and the love and support of a friend is priceless.

Friends are one of the most wonderful gifts and it is through them that Jesus is revealed. During that year, friends were my lifeline to healing. They rolled out the red carpet and accompanied me on my journey. When I was tired and just couldn't go on, Jesus was there with them to carry me the rest of the way. I am here because they were there for me. God provided for my needs. Of that, there is NO doubt!

RITA CARBUHN

THE 12th SIGN: THIRST NO MORE

"As the deer pants for streams of water, so my soul pants for you, O God. My soul thirsts for God, for the living God. When can I go and meet with God?" (Psalms 42:1-2, NIV)

Water, the life-giving element that is a major part of our bodies and earth, is something we take for granted. We often lose sight of how precious it is!

For Christians, water takes on a spiritual significance. It represents our baptism, our commitment to the Lord, and our union with Jesus. We are told if we drink of His water, we will thirst no more. We will be filled to the point of overflowing and be whole. When I didn't feel whole because of my cancer and mastectomy, this promise was even more appealing. We always seem to yearn for the things we cannot have; however, God's truth is a gift we can have whenever we desire. If we surrender to Him, He will ALWAYS deliver on His promises.

Throughout the year, I was given His water daily. He served me and I drank eagerly. I honestly don't know how people deal with cancer if they don't have a belief in our omnipotent God. Even possessing a strong faith, I found the journey to be a long and tortuous one. I was never guaranteed that my Christian life would be smooth and free of pain, but that was my expectation once I professed my love for the Lord. Although the Bible says to expect suffering and persecution, I didn't truly comprehend its meaning. That said, it didn't take long to realize my expectations were unrealistic and simply wrong.

All of us have dark valleys through which we must travel in this journey called "life" and it is during those times that Jesus gives us the opportunity to grow in our trust of Him. When I realized there was no other option than facing that dark valley, I knew I would be facing my toughest challenge. There was no turning back. The interesting part is Jesus revealed inner resources and strength in myself that I didn't know existed. That is His pattern; when we are weak, He gives us strength. He spoke to my heart in new ways and I heard his voice differently. I developed a spiritual vision that enabled me to see through the murkiness. It was as if I had specially-equipped goggles to distinguish the shape of the landscape in that darkness. This is what faith is all about. Barbara Johnson, author of *Stick a Geranium in Your Hat*, said it well. "Faith is seeing light with your heart when all your eyes see is the darkness ahead." By the end of my journey, I found a new level of contentment for life. Joy saturated my being and I have continued to be filled daily with God's joy! I survived and now celebrate the special gift and wonderment of LIFE.

Water played an interesting role in my healing. Immediately after the mastectomy, when I couldn't shower because of the surgical drain, I longed for the impossible. Even though I took daily baths, they didn't satisfy me. I looked forward to showering. In my mind, that act was associated with wholeness. When I was finally able to shower, I allowed the water to run over my body for about forty-five minutes and it was mesmerizing!

During that first shower post-op, I was transcended to another reality. It was as if Jesus himself was pouring His water over me and assuring me I was healed. He held me in His arms and bathed me in the same way He washed the feet of His disciples! I was filled to the point of overflowing with His tenderness, love, and compassion. Jesus took on the role of being a servant to me! *Why would He do this for me? I am only one of His many children in the world, so why would He want to show me this level of His love? This is awesome!*

That experience repeated itself daily throughout the six months of chemo. Honestly, I didn't want to leave the shower, even though my skin was shriveling like a prune! The water became the healing power of Jesus! By allowing it to saturate my skin completely, I felt electrified by the Holy Spirit. My body was being restored! However, when I saw the water bills, it was something else! My lengthy showers were not cheap! I hoped this "shower experience" would never leave me because it was a reminder of my renewal and rebirth. I didn't want to lose the unique awareness of Jesus' presence. Sadly, the intensity of my feelings faded, but my awareness of God's compassion has not. I am reminded of His magnificence and compassion each and every time I step into my shower. I know I am on Holy ground!

The fact I took my vacation at the beach did not go unnoticed. If the water was so healing in my shower, then it made sense that being in and near the ocean would have an even greater impact. Of course, I didn't know this when I planned the vacation, but isn't it interesting how all the pieces fit so beautifully together? In the past, I have always felt somewhat irritated with the salt and sand from the beach. It made me feel sticky and dirty. I could hardly wait to wash it off at the day's end. However, during that special vacation with Bonnie, the ocean held a different experience. I felt cleansed. When I took a dip in the water, I felt renewed and refreshed because Jesus was there. He and

I played together in the surf, rode the waves, and splashed each other with water. When I lost my footing and the current was about to carry me away from the shore, He steadied me with His hand. Even when I was walking on the shore and the water flowed around my feet, I felt His healing power flow into my body. There was a sense of oneness with my Lord and Savior, which words cannot adequately describe. His tranquility and peace surrounded me and the valley of that shadowy darkness didn't exist for that week.

Water continued to play a significant role in my recovery after I returned from my vacation. During my last month of chemo, when I vomited almost endlessly, I couldn't tolerate even small sips of water. I longed for a drink, but when I took one, I would vomit more. I tried to quench my desire by coating my lips with ice. It helped a little, but what I really wanted was a cool drink. I then understood what Jesus experienced when he was in the wilderness for forty days. I felt as if I was roaming in that desert, too. As strange as it sounds, I thought if I didn't get some of that life-giving water, I wouldn't make it out of the desert alive. So, I poured a glass of water and carried it around the house. I looked at it frequently as a reminder of what it represented. At night, I placed it on the nightstand by my bed. Perhaps it sounds a little crazy, but I would hold the glass of water, smell it, and examine it thoroughly, in minute detail.

Then, the unexpected happened.

One day, I saw Jesus' face smiling back at me! I was shocked! At the same time, it provided comfort and soothed my soul. This "vision experience" with Jesus continued for the last three months of my chemo, which was when I needed His presence more than ever. Once the treatments were completed, His face disappeared from that glass. I was sad, but I also understood I no longer needed that level of support.

Those last three months were the most trying times of my journey with cancer. I was at my lowest point and realized I was desperately in need of some of visible reminders of Jesus' compassion. When my friends developed the idea of having prayer vigils, they shared both the times and names of those praying. I posted this list on my refrigerator so I could check it frequently, as it was another thing that comforted me. Once again, the unexpected occurred—I was provided with a prompting of the person's name or with a vision of the person praying! Initially, it frightened me, but when I realized what was happening, it became another awesome gift! It was one more way in which

Jesus communicated His presence. He was providing everything I needed.

My Spiritual Lesson:

Symbols are very important. They surround us in all aspects of our lives and are essential in helping us remember a variety of people, places, and things. When I was in the darkest hours of my journey and felt lost and alone, the symbol of water provided the blessed assurance of God's love. When I looked at that water, I knew Jesus was there!

"If anyone is thirsty, let him come to me and drink. Whoever believes in me, as the Scripture has said, streams of living water will flow from within him." (John 7:37-38, NIV)

RITA CARBUHN

THE 13th SIGN: LICKS AND PROMISES

"Rejoice in the Lord always. I will say it again: Rejoice! Let your gentleness be evident to all. The Lord is near. Do not be anxious about anything, but in everything by prayer and petition, with thanksgiving, present your requests to God. And the peace of God, which transcends all understanding, will guard your hearts and your minds in Christ Jesus." (Philippians 4:4-7, NIV)

Dogs have always been an important part of my life. When I was small and lived on a farm, I was surrounded by all the animals I ever wanted, but there were never enough dogs! We usually had at least two. One dog, however, completely captured my heart. Pepper was a German Shepherd and Collie crossbreed, and was 6 weeks old when we got him. His name came from his mix of brown and black hair. Pepper was our devoted playmate, rarely separated from my brother and me.

One day, he was hit by a tractor and his leg was broken. Dad set the leg and nursed him back to health because there wasn't money for a veterinarian. I don't think Pepper was ever quite the same afterwards. He always had a bit of a limp, but it never prevented him from being active. He was fiercely protective of us. All our neighbors knew this, too. He growled at anyone who came to our farm, even if he knew them from previous visits. On more than one occasion, he saved us from harm. Both before and after his leg injury, Pepper was a typical, outdoor farm dog. At night, when we went inside, he would wander. It was during one of these night escapades that Pepper was shot and killed by a neighbor. When he didn't show up at the farm for several days, we knew something wasn't right. My brother and I found him lying in a ditch as we walked to school. That was my first experience in losing a beloved dog and it was definitely traumatic for me.

When we moved to town, Dad refused to get another dog. He believed they should only be outdoors and a city yard was not appropriate. Regardless of how much I begged, he firmly denied my pleas, so I ended up befriending all of the neighbors' dogs and filling my bedroom with stuffed animals (mostly dogs and puppies!). I became a version the "Pied Piper" in our neighborhood. Whenever I went anywhere, I had a group of dogs trailing me. I knew every dog within a four-block radius of our house by name and regularly played with each one.

I looked forward to the day when I could have my own dog.

My dream of having a canine companion came true after I purchased my first house. At first, I couldn't decide on a breed. Since my house was small, it was important to get a dog that was small enough, who could be managed in my limited space. One evening, my boyfriend told me a puppy was found on his porch that noon. I asked what happened to it since it was an unusually cold night. When I learned he did nothing, I insisted we check on it. I envisioned a large puppy, the size of my German shepherd; however, what I found was a very small, mixed breed puppy I could hold in one hand! It was obvious she was too small to maneuver the steps to his porch. Someone had purposefully placed her there! The only response was to adopt her for the night. That "night" lasted for the next 15 years!

I named the dog Goldie because her free spirit reminded me of the actress, Goldie Hawn! She clearly had a mind of her own. In the first two years, I wasn't sure which of us was going to survive. Her puppyhood was very trying. I lost more shoes and articles of clothing from her chewing than I care to admit. I loved her sense of freedom, but she was oblivious to the dangerousness passing cars posed, so we walked in a protected park. We were joined by 10 other dogs and 8 owners during our daily walks, and the fellowship among all us and all of our pets was absolutely delightful. Our group became very close and we began sharing meals on Friday evenings. We ended up naming ourselves the Dog Food Club! Watching the dogs interact was such fun. Usually, Goldie would stay with the group for 10 minutes and then would explore on her own. She made the rounds to the homes whose backyards abutted the park, so everyone knew her. It was a great opportunity to meet my neighbors because she would seek out those who were grilling or having a picnic. I would find her begging for food when I finally joined them. I ate more burgers, hot dogs, and birthday cakes while searching for her than ever before in my life! She certainly knew how to network and it was always for food!

Goldie was a "Heinz 57 variety" with a lot of Wire Fox Terrier in her. Although she was tan when her hair was short, her hair became curly, all white, and wiry in nature as it grew longer. The hair on her ears fell into wavy locks about three inches below the ear. The top portion of her ear was tan, but the longer hairs were white. A friend of mine called her a Disney dog. Indeed, she looked like she should be in the movies! She loved people and was very affectionate. She would kiss you until you would beg her to stop. Her friendliness changed instantly, however, if she thought someone would harm me. She took her job as my watchdog seriously and was extremely protective. I really appreciated this quality because I lived alone and liked having her warn me. Even the mailman couldn't believe she was so little the first time he saw her. He was sure I had a Doberman attacking the door when he delivered the mail!

One fall, she began to act strangely. She became afraid of others and didn't want to be touched. For such a loving dog, this was very odd. I took her to the vet, who diagnosed her with loneliness.

"She needs a companion," he said. *I'm not sure I can handle a second dog. This one is quite enough!*

Shortly after that, my neighbor found a dog wandering around the neighborhood she believed would be a perfect companion for Goldie. It was a sweet, black Cockapoo, about three to four months old. I fell in love with her instantly! However, I wanted to have a trial period of a week with the two, before making a final decision. Honestly, that was a week from hell; they fought all the time! When I hit my limit with their fighting, I told the Cockapoo I was returning her the next morning. To my surprise, the two dogs bonded that night and ended up being virtually inseparable. I kept Munchkin, and nicknamed her Munchies, due to her small size. The two were so cute. They slept together, ate from the same bowl, and ran together in the park. Goldie's personality returned to her former affectionate self. Life was good.

Five months later, Munchies was hit by a car and subsequently died in my arms. My heart was broken. Both Goldie and I felt lost and wondered what's next.

God understood our broken hearts and knew what was needed, but all I could think about was grieving my loss.

A couple of months later, an opportunity presented itself. One of my friends had a guide dog she was trying to place. She believed Murdoch was the perfect answer for my—our—loneliness.

I was ecstatic!

Murdoch and Goldie already knew each other, so I was certain it would be a good arrangement. It was. Murdoch, Goldie, and I became a family and we all shared a special bond. God didn't make the accident happen with Munchies, but He clearly used the opportunity to help us move in another direction that was equally as beneficial. What seemed like a negative with the loss of

Munchies became a positive with the addition of our newest family member.

Murdoch was a delightfully funny dog! Although he was very intelligent, he acted as though he wasn't. His actions and behavior were hilarious. I called him my original, stand-up comedian. His bark was a "woo-woo" and sounded more like a train. He was not like the typical Retriever who wants to fetch sticks or balls. He saw his role in life as one of exploring and roaming about the neighborhood or sleeping and eating. He was the neighborhood greeter and took that task seriously. He had a definite preference for men. Unfortunately, I was never able to train him to search for a single, eligible man for me! I think Murdoch took his job as a "seeing eye" dog literally, because he was always content to watch the world go by. He truly enjoyed being more of a spectator than a participant. He was very large, with good markings, and had a handsome coat of long, wavy, dark red hair. He was one of the most beautiful Golden Retrievers I have ever seen. Even more important was how much I loved this dog. He was an answer to my prayers!

My dogs have been my family and support system for years. They became my children and have been afforded a comfortable life. I spent many hours with them—walking, playing, and cuddling with them daily. They brought me such pleasure and certainly deserved my love and attention in return. If I had errands to run, they accompanied me, when the weather permitted. They went to my friends' homes and were as much a part of their lives as mine. Many of my activities were dog-oriented, including birthday parties, Christmas gatherings, etc. Pictures of us were part of the church directory and others accepted my dogs as my family. When I transferred my membership to the Kentucky church, the dogs were listed as members, too. Mother and Dad always received cards and letters from their grandchildren (my dogs) and every letter was signed by the dogs' paw prints.

There is no doubt that dogs are a spiritual gift from God. They offer unconditional love, every day of their lives. It doesn't make any difference how I feel or look or if I am having a good or bad day. Like God, they love me anyway. Their love and faithfulness are the only constants in an ever-changing world.

With their affectionate looks, their licks of love, and their companionship, they have always been available to minister to my needs and create a special kind of joy.

I know God has blessed me with their presence and I am ever so thankful.

Throughout my illness, my dogs suffered greatly. Since I was unable to walk them daily, as was our pattern, they became confused and frustrated. They begged to go on walks, but I couldn't comply. My visitors took them out, but I didn't have anyone to do that routinely. Interestingly, Murdoch developed an eye infection with my very first chemo treatment. So did I.

Despite treatment for both of us, our infections didn't disappear until I finished my entire treatment series. I was convinced Murdoch's eye problems demonstrated the bond we had. Unfortunately, the illnesses didn't stop there. He was then diagnosed with liver and pancreas infections and became seriously ill. I was worried I was going to lose him. Amazingly, he recovered fully.

Then it was Goldie's turn. All throughout the chemo, she would shiver and shake until I picked her up and placed her on my chest to calm down. With her head resting on my shoulder, she would fall asleep, listening to my heart. Even though she stopped eating and lost half her weight, I was able to nurse her back to health. Neither dog would let me out of sight. When I was vomiting, they stayed beside me until I stopped. Whenever I slept, both dogs snuggled beside me. Goldie always had a special sense when I was upset and crying. She would rush to my side even before I made a sound and then lick away my tears.

God understood what I didn't. He served me well. He knew if I lost either dog during my chemo, I would have given up. In fact, when I was first diagnosed, I entertained the possibility of putting my dogs to sleep and burying them with me if I were to die. I couldn't bear the thought of leaving them behind, not knowing where they would be. Both were older, so adjusting to a new environment would be a challenge.

I agonized and cried for hours over the mere thought. Fortunately, I didn't have to face that issue. The Lord helped me grow stronger before He handed me that dilemma. In January of the following year, Goldie began growing weaker and refused to eat. Lab tests showed she was suffering from a liver infection with tumors present. Even a course of antibiotics didn't help her improve. More tests and X-rays showed the tumors were growing and nothing could be done. Surgery didn't make sense. She was two months shy of sixteen and I didn't want to cause her more pain. Her health declined quickly and I watched for signs when I needed to make that dreaded final decision. One Saturday morning, I took her for her last walk. She was weary and could hardly move.

It was obvious she was in pain. I carried her more than halfway home. I knew the day had come.

On a cold and snowy day in March, I said goodbye to my baby, Goldie. It broke my heart because she had been such an important part of my life. She wasn't just a dog; she was part of me! In fact, Murdoch and I both lost part of our hearts that day. However, I'm sure we will all be reunited in heaven.

My Spiritual Lesson:

I learned that Jesus knows our needs before we do, and so provides for us. In my case, He knew I could not handle euthanizing either of my dogs during my chemo treatments.

During the times of illness (on my part or theirs), things were simply overwhelming. *I don't want to live without my babies and I don't want them to be without me! I can't go on if something happens to them! Lord, let us go together! Bury me with them!*

Thanks to Jesus, I didn't have to face that decision.

I had so many blessings during those terrible times. Friends accompanied me to the vet and assisted with Goldie's burial. I couldn't have handled that task alone. Jesus also knew I would need additional support and assistance in the days following her death.

I had made prior arrangements to attend an incredible spirit-filled weekend called the Walk to Emmaus. It just so "happened" to be scheduled six days after I put Goldie down. Isn't God amazing? I didn't want to go because I felt so sad and lost, but my sponsors encouraged me to attend. They convinced me it was the perfect place to be and they were so right! During that weekend, I was surrounded with unconditional love. Jesus joined me on the walk, cried with me in my loss, soothed my grief-filled days and nights, and held me in His arms to tell me I was loved. I know He held Goldie in His arms, too.

THE 14th SIGN: WITH PEN IN HAND

"Be still and know that I am God." (Psalms 46:10, NIV)

From the beginning of my journey with cancer, I had an unexplainable compulsion to record my thoughts and feelings. I couldn't understand why this feeling was so strong because writing was not an activity I maintained on a consistent basis. I would keep a journal for a while and stop, then pick it up again and stop later. This cycle was familiar. My intention was always to keep a daily diary, but it would be set aside, due to other priorities.

However, this time, something felt different, and I began recording things before I went to bed each night. I kept pens and paper by my bed as well as a recorder. Even on those nights when I was too tired to write or tape, I had the amazing ability to recall my thoughts in detail the next morning so I could record them. I know the Lord was helping me work through my struggles in this way. I believed I would be asked to share my experience with cancer, although I had no idea how, when, where, or with whom.

The ability to write has always been something I have enjoyed. Usually, it had been in the form of reports, research papers,

213

and business plans rather than the more creative forms of short stories, poetry, and books. However, I have discovered that, whenever I am in a crisis, writing has provided a useful outlet. It became a way to express my feelings in a safe and constructive way while also affording me the opportunity to learn from my experience. It made sense to journal when I was facing the most difficult struggle of my life.

My written words took on an energy of their own. Poetry flowed from deep within me in ways I never knew existed. It became the means for my sorrow and grief as well as for my praise and thanksgiving. I was often astounded with what emerged. Thoughts and ideas came at any time of the day or night. My mind was so active that, when I was unable to sleep, I would journal my thoughts. For some reason, I didn't judge the merit of my words. Rather, I just allowed them to flow. I believed the Holy Spirit was actively working within my heart and what was being revealed was something I needed to examine.

Writing gave me a sense of control over what I was experiencing, which was a wonderful gift from the Holy Spirit. So much of what I was going through made me feel powerless, so I desperately needed this gift. I found it very difficult to face each day without having some great miracle happening in my life, but the surprise was that a miracle was taking place within my heart! I was learning to rely on the Lord and recognizing His power in my life. Control was an issue with which I have struggled for most of my life. However, through my experience with cancer, I saw a gradual yielding of myself to the Lord. "Surrender" is what He encouraged me to do and it was what I had to do, on most days, to exist. I knew my life had literally been placed in His hands and all I could do was rest in Him.

Interestingly, as I wrote about the Lord, I found that my relationship with Him became more vibrant and alive. I always felt He was trying to open my eyes to the events and relationships around me, but the primary focus was our relationship. I never expected the outcome of this experience to be a more intimate relationship with Jesus, but that was exactly what happened.

He was present for every step of my journey. He walked with me when I was weak and couldn't walk on my own. He held me when I needed comfort. He listened to my complaints and pleadings. He helped me pray when I had no words to utter.

The intimacy in our relationship was palpable and so very precious. It was unlike anything I had ever experienced and something that is so difficult to describe in words. And yet, writing for the Lord is a powerful and purposeful action!

I don't know why He has chosen me for this task, but I believe I am expected to share my testimony.

My Spiritual Lesson:

I actually learned many lessons, including these 25:

1. Life is never empty or lonely if Jesus is kept in the #1 position.
2. When we come to the end of ourselves, God begins.
3. If you love yourself, then loving others comes more easily.
4. When God leads, He always strengthens.
5. God gave us a will to make loving and living more meaningful.
6. Keep our eyes on God and nothing can keep us from His peace.
7. In the stillness, He speaks.
8. When the darkness surrounds us, He is beside us.
9. When you cry, He cries, too.
10. He follows through with His promises.
11. He wants to be our best friend.
12. He loves each of us for who we are.

13. He is present with us every day, in every way, of our lives.
14. His plan for our lives far exceeds anything we could fashion for ourselves.
15. If we trust in God, there is no reason to worry, for He will satisfy our every need.
16. Living only has meaning if you are invested in Jesus and live for Him.
17. Only when we are in the danger of losing something do we realize its real value.
18. True power is seeing life from His perspective and living His will.
19. He provides us with tools we need to do His work.
20. When we work for the glory of God, miracles happen.
21. He always moves us in new directions.
22. He alone knows how we can be of best use to Him.
23. He uses every opportunity to teach us about Him and His ways.
24. Life is a very precious gift from God.
25. The Lord wants us to witness for Him daily in every thought, word, action, and deed.

THE 15th SIGN: A, E, I, O, AND ALWAYS U, LORD

"If you accept my words and store up my commands within you, turning your ear to wisdom and applying your heart to understanding and if you call out for insight, and cry aloud for understanding… then you will understand the fear of the Lord and find the knowledge of God. For the Lord gives wisdom, and from His mouth comes knowledge and understanding." (Proverbs 2:1-6, NIV)

I have always loved books and enjoyed reading. This interest was nurtured by my parents when I was small, and is one which my brother and I share.

Once our chores were completed on the farm, the evening was a time for relaxation. We listened to radio programs or spent time reading. It was a time I remember my father or mother reading to me. If we ran out of materials, then Mother would invent the most interesting stories. I always thought she was so clever and I delighted in what she created. Both my parents were quite intelligent, even though neither of them went to college. Dad was forced out of school after sixth grade because his parents needed him to work on their farm. Sadly, he was treated more like a hired hand in his family while his sister was given other options. Mother completed both high school and business school to prepare for her job at Hartford Insurance.

Because of their personal experiences, both emphasized the importance of a college degree.

"Get an education. No one can ever take that away from you."

I heard this repeatedly.

Dad talked about it more than Mother, but she was just as supportive. Reading and studying were always a priority in our family. When I was in high school, the emphasis was on good grades and studying hard. If I brought "A"s home, I had as much freedom as I wanted. Of course, to get the "A"s, I had to study hard, so I didn't waste my time in foolish ways. That satisfied my father tremendously.

My friends knew how much I loved to read. During my treatment, they supplied me with all kinds of reading materials. I was given a variety, from romance novels and self-help books to cancer testimonials and almost anything in between. I was particularly interested in the materials that spoke to health and healing, whether it was secular or religious. I devoured everything I was given. I was particularly interested in the stories of others who were dealing with cancer because I gained hope and encouragement from them. However, some were too graphic and I identified with their pain. I quickly put those stories aside. Others were filled with facts and statistics about cancer and simply were boring. When I read them, I felt like I was dying and there was no hope for a future. I tried reading books about chemo, but they made me physically ill and I realized that was not in my best interest.

The books that offered suggestions on how to maintain a positive outlook and attitude were extremely helpful because I felt that was what I needed the most during this journey.

Without question, the most significant book was the Bible. (This should come as no surprise!) It provided me with the most amount of comfort and hope. I read story after story of those who had suffered pain and loss. Even though I was reading about events that took place thousands of years ago, there were things I learned from each story. The Book of Psalms spoke to my suffering and anguish. I never realized how much total despair the psalmists spoke of until I was caught in my own darkness.

Suddenly, I was the one who was hurting and crying out for the Lord's help!

There were so many days when I didn't know what to read. I let the pages fall open and then read where I was led. It always contained something that was pertinent. I felt as though God was trying to reveal one of His truths by leading me to that scripture. Philippians taught me about joy, which I desperately needed. The Book of Isaiah was filled with numerous songs of praise and thanksgiving. I found hope in His promises contained there.

"But those that trust in the Lord for help will find their strength renewed. They will rise on wings like eagles; they will run and not get weary; they will walk and not grow weak." (Isaiah 40:31, Good News Study Bible)

Reading the many verses in Isaiah which formed the lyrics in Handel's *Messiah* also renewed my faith and soothed my soul. Then I realized my story was nothing compared to Jesus' crucifixion. His story was clearly THE story of pain and anguish!

Books authored by cancer survivors were extremely helpful. I learned what actions were beneficial during their treatment as well as which ones weren't. I also found their struggles similar to mine and they provided me with support and comfort. It was easier to read about their struggles than to focus on mine. Gradually, as I read their personal stories, I began to understand my own fears and anxieties better. I gained mastery over what I perceived as an impossible and uncontrollable personal situation. I also became better able to deal with the flood of thoughts and emotions I experienced. This knowledge, along with changes I made, placed me firmly on the road to recovery.

My readings helped me learn new ways to cope with my cancer. I wanted to be able to manage my cancer in the same manner I had been able to handle other adversities. I had always taken pride in my resilience. I saw this situation as no different but, I have to admit, I was still reeling from the diagnosis. Nonetheless, I read books by cancer specialists, Dr. O. Carl Simonton and Dr. Bernie Siegel, and implemented some of their techniques such as visualizations, guided imagery, creative writing, and art drawings. The visualization and guided imagery exercises were useful to de-stress. I loved the peace and tranquility that I achieved using these techniques. The doctors also recommended the use of relaxation and meditation exercises, to promote a healing environment. I had used them with my patients, so I was familiar with the techniques, but now I needed them for my own healing. I found they provided the means to reduce the high stress levels I had. I started using them daily, in the evenings, as a way to empty my mind of my worries and stress from each day. I began making my own relaxation tapes and used those with a religious focus, as they were most beneficial. I also found it useful to spend quiet time meditating on individual Bible verses. That time alone with God was not only relaxing, but it also helped me be more open and receptive to His presence. And the intimacy between Jesus and me became even more precious.

The visualization exercises also had a purpose other than the obvious one of relaxation. In my readings, I was challenged to make a drawing or painting that represented my view of cancer and its treatment. Being a visually-oriented person and an artist in my own right, I thought this would be an easy assignment. However, I struggled for days and just couldn't come up with an image that was appropriate. I was puzzled why this process was so difficult. I prayed for God to give me an image. It was suggested by a friend to trust God with the process and just start drawing to see what would emerge. So, that is what I did. Suddenly, there was a picture of a river, which represented God's transforming light flowing into my body. The light was very bright, white, and translucent. I visualized the light drowning the cancer cells when they came in contact with one another. In this way, the cancer cells could easily be "carried off" to a repository outside of my body and no longer affect me. Just as we are unable to look directly into the face of God, these cells were affected in the same way. Their power was destroyed by the overwhelming brightness of God's light. This image was very powerful and comforting because I felt as though I was personally being cared for by Jesus. While receiving my chemo, I used this image to increase my power in overcoming the cancer. Some days, the image made me feel like I was impervious to the disease. When those days came, I knew I was going to be triumphant in my battle. I felt on top of the world. There were other days when the healing image wasn't useful and when I couldn't be sustained for even a few minutes. When that happened, I just leaned on the Lord and asked for His grace and mercy. He never disappointed me! This image, my painting, actually appears on the cover of this book! I have included other paintings I did in the pages that follow the last chapter of this book, too.

Although the mind is powerful, it wasn't until I finished reading Norman Vincent Peale's book, *The Power of Positive Thinking*, that I realized how important it was in terms of my personal healing. I read story after story of various people who, in addition to their traditional western medical treatments and therapies, had moved into healing through prayer and positive thinking. I was very curious how they could sustain their strong positive thoughts to overcome their infirmities. *What qualities do they have that I don't possess? How come it works with some people and not others? Is the difference in how much one believes? Or is it something else? Do I have what it takes?* As I studied in more detail, I realized prayer was essential in maintaining a positive outlook. I could make changes to achieve healthy living, but if I didn't transform my negative thoughts of guilt and shame into positive thoughts, I was sabotaging myself. For me, FAITH IN GOD was an essential part of this process.

Then I recalled the story of Jesus walking on the water. As He walked toward His disciples, He tried to calm them by saying, "Courage. It is I. Don't be afraid." When Peter questioned Him, Jesus ordered him to come to Him. Peter obeyed and walked on the water until he suddenly lost his focus and became fearful. That is when he began to sink. Jesus reached out to save him, but also asked him, "What little faith you have! Why did you doubt?" I thought to myself how much I was sounding like Peter through my entire cancer experience. I doubted my own faith in God's miraculous healing powers. How foolish was I being?

My Spiritual Lesson:

I wish it were possible to remove all the negative thoughts from our minds while we live on this earth. I can only imagine how exciting and wonderful life would be if only unconditional love surrounded us every moment. What a magical world this would be! Isn't that what God intended to have happen with the Garden of Eden in the first place? Oh, what we have lost!

Jesus lived His life with the power of positive thinking. Anything was possible. He tried to teach this concept to His disciples and get them to understand these powers were also available to them if they believed, too! Our beliefs are our realities! Who am I to question the powers of my Lord? I think about how life will be when Jesus returns and rules the earth for eternity. Oh, how I look forward to those days!

RITA CARBUHN

THE 16th SIGN: WITNESSING IS BELIEVING

"Continue to work out your salvation with fear and trembling, for it is God who works in you to will and to act according to His good purpose. Do everything without complaining or arguing, so that you may become blameless and pure children of God without fault in a crooked and depraved generation, in which you shine like stars in the universe as you hold out the word of life—in order that I may boast on the day of Christ that I did not run or labor for nothing." (Philippians 2:14-16, NIV)

My story—my spiritual journey with cancer—is simply a love story. It is one which tells of a God whose love is so powerful that it transforms lives forever! It was a distant story until His love touched my life and transformed me.

At that point, I fully understood what it meant to be a precious child of God! Yes, I am the daughter of the King, a princess, and the bride of Christ. This is an incredible love that is so hard to define, but it is a story that needs to be told, and telling others is what I am expected to do.

I don't know how long I will live.

At the time of this writing, I believe my cancer is under control, but there is no way to know, other than letting the years pass. However, I choose to believe God has blessed me with one of his awesome miracles! And I am forever thankful!

Despite the fact that life on this earth is very brief, I am convinced that most of us don't take the best advantage of it. We get sidetracked by meaningless struggles with our egos, power, control, winning, and material gains. We are driven by false relationships and our own sexual desires. We lose sight of the special gift of having relationships with others and of the opportunities to witness our Lord. We overlook the power of His love and fail to realize its major significance in our lives. Most of all, we fail to acknowledge how critical our reliance on God actually is and, instead, deceive ourselves into thinking we can do it all. Whatever the case, we have to recognize we are human and, at our core, we are all sinners! We cannot expect ourselves to achieve Christ's level of perfection. Yet, we should strive for it. When we fall short, which we do and will do daily, we need to repent and ask for forgiveness. Then we need to try again!

We will repeat this pattern many times throughout our lives. There should never be a time when we cease to strive to be more like Jesus.

As a result of my cancer experience, I am trying to live differently. I reach out toward others in more loving ways and share my feelings openly. I find myself praying for my enemies and asking for healing in their hearts. Interestingly, God always seems to put a twist on it. More often than not, it is my heart that is healed instead—my attitude changes and suddenly I find I am more tolerant of my enemy.

My goal is to honor Jesus in all I do and to bring Him glory. I have found the peace that surpasses all understanding. There is joy and contentment in my life. I believe all of this is possible because I am walking closer with my Lord. I have been given a second chance at life and, this time, I am trying NOT to waste my efforts. At the same time, I find myself yearning for Jesus' return. I know I am living in the "last days" and believe the Rapture will come soon. Needless to say, I am looking forward to when I see Jesus!

My Spiritual Lesson:

I am reminded of Moses' words: "Remember what you have learned about the Lord through your experiences with him. It was you, not your children, who had these experiences… teach them to your children" (Deuteronomy 11:19).

I believe God wants me to share the lessons I have learned through my experience and spiritual journey with cancer because there is information in them that can benefit others. Whether the process is a formal or informal one, a large group of people or one person, in written form or verbally, it makes no difference. I am simply asked to share my testimony. Some people who hear my story will be facing the threat of cancer, but others may be facing a different demon. We all face trials and can learn from each other's experiences, regardless of the reason. I know I can share hope and encouragement and I certainly understand loneliness. There is no question I have been through the darkness, but the point of my story is the glorious light that awaits us on the other side. This is a story that needs to be told!

Death is something I have learned to cherish and accept. When there is acceptance with death, there is freedom in living. It doesn't mean I want to die tomorrow, but I know that, when my day comes, I will surely be more accepting of it.

I have prepared myself by how I have lived since my cancer diagnosis. At the same time, I don't want to be complacent. There is always more I can do to be like Jesus, and to tell others about Him. Witnessing is what we are directed to do. Jesus gave us that command in The Great Commission. So, my plan is to move forward with purpose for Jesus!

If you have been touched in any way while reading this book, I ask that you, too, share my experience with others. It may help them bring comfort and support to someone who needs it, including themselves.

"Therefore, go and make disciples of all nations, baptizing them in the name of the Father, and of the Son, and of the Holy Spirit, and teaching them to obey everything I have commanded to you. And surely, I am with you always, to the very end of the age." (Matthew 28:19-20, NIV)

RITA CARBUHN

Special Words from the Author

First...

This book has been the result of a 25-year journey! In 1993, I was diagnosed with cancer. As you have read, that was followed by a mastectomy and six months of chemo. By Thanksgiving, I was pronounced cancer-free!

During the next year, I wrote my manuscript using the recordings and writings I created during my treatment. I was convinced the Holy Spirit was urging me to get it published, so that became the next step.

Although I tried the traditional route, my efforts only yielded a stack of rejection letters. Feeling discouraged, I decided to take a break, but I still continued to refine my manuscript with the hope that something would materialize in the future. Over the years, I explored other options, but nothing came of my efforts. Then, in 2018, I met a woman who had published a book herself. She strongly encouraged me to explore this option.

Again, the unexpected happened! Two months later, a self-publishing opportunity arose! In the words of Steve Harvey, a well-known comedian and talk show host, I

"JUMPED" and what you are holding in your hands is the outcome of that leap!

Herein lies yet another spiritual lesson: God's timing is always perfect! My dream was fulfilled as I celebrated being a 25-year cancer survivor! Happy Birthday, Rita! Praise be to God!

Second...

While on my journey of healing, I looked for therapeutic ways to express my feelings. Music, writing, and art became my therapy. It was my way to gain mastery over a situation that felt completely out of my control.

I soon learned being able to express my feelings, whether positive or negative, was extremely important to my healing. These next few pages contain some of my writings, poetry, and artwork.

In addition to the reference I made in Chapter 11: The 11th Sign, about the image (my painting) that appears on the cover of this book, I have also included a few sentences about what each piece of artwork included in the pages that follow represents and means to me.

TO MY FRIEND, FRIEDA

This poem was written as a memorial to my friend, Frieda. Since I was unable to attend her service, a friend read this at her funeral.

To My Friend, Frieda

I have loved you like a mother,
From the moment we first met.
The joy and love you radiated,
I believe, were heaven-sent.

You brightened up the darkest room,
With your light from above.
And whenever I was feeling down and out,
You touched me with your love.

Oh, the stories that we shared
Among our "Chatterstitch" clan,
The laughter, smiles, and sorrows
Were all part of God's great plan!

You have been the finest example
Of God's unconditional love and giving.
Your faith in Him never seemed to waver,
Nor did your zest for living.

Frieda, I'm so very sorry.
The miles kept me from your side.
I would have told you, "I love you,"
And together, we could have said
"Goodbye."

Somehow, I suspect you knew
How much I truly cared.
And all my feelings, thoughts, and dreams,
You and I have already shared.

My grief and sadness are comforted today,
Knowing that you are now "home,"
And with you as my "guardian angel,"
I will never need to feel alone.

TO THE SHARE GROUP

This was written as a "Thank you" to my Christian share group along. I gave it, along with a gift of a hematite cross, to each member. I was honored with their visits and prayers while I was hospitalized, and was gifted with all kinds of books, audiotapes, and videos once I came home.

Most of all, I treasured the laughter and love we shared, which were key ingredients in my healing process. Through their friendships and support, I began to feel "whole" again. Their prayers carried me through my turmoil and struggles.

I thank God for their love and compassion and felt very privileged to call them my friends. God blessed me enormously with their presence in my life.

To the Share Group

To have Christian friends like you,
Who truly love and care,
Is one of God's wonderful treasures
That I am blessed to share.

I am comforted to know
That each of you is there.
For when the darkness fell upon me,
I was overcome with despair.

But your love and concern
Helped me through the difficult days.
I know your prayers were heard,
For God's healing works in many ways.

This little, hematite cross,
So shiny and so new,
Is my way of thanking God
For each one of you.

I hope when you wear it
You are reminded of our sharing,
And that a group such as ours
Is God's special way of caring.

Thank you!

ODE TO MY BREAST!

One day, I was moved to write a poem that was basically a "farewell" to my breast. I decided that if I was to accept losing my breast, I had to grieve its loss. Grieving meant saying "Goodbye," and it is out of that realization and my pain that this poem emerged.

I wrote this when I was in a somber mood and it was meant to be taken seriously, but when I shared it with my mother, she erupted in a fit of laughter.

"This is the funniest thing I have ever read!"

Her comments hurt my feelings. I told her it was serious and her laughing upset me.

Her reply was, "Rita, you have to loosen up. You will adjust and be fine. It's only a breast, not your life. You will come to see the humor in this poem, too."

She was right. As I progressed in my healing journey, I was able to share the laughter with this verse, too.

Ode to My Breast!

From very early on
You, breasts, were always small.
I often used to question
If you were even there at all.

I always hoped and wished
You would increase in size,
But no potions, lotions, or creams
Would make you grow, in my eyes.

I used to joke and tease
That, "A training bra is all I need."
I hoped that you would finally develop
When I passed through puberty.

But puberty came and went,
And you never really changed…
Except, surprisingly, to become droopy
And sag, the older I became.

Whenever I gained any weight,
Suddenly, I felt you, as real breasts.
You would jiggle, move, and bounce.
Wow! I had "boobs" on my chest!

It is interesting to me
That, of you, I would joke,

Only to be diagnosed with cancer.
Truly now, this is no hoax!

I cried, but also thought and said,
"Without you, I can live!"
My identity is not based on you;
There is more of me to give.

And so, the mastectomy, I had,
On the twentieth of May this year.
And now, I see life differently…
Especially the things I hold so dear.

You, breasts, have now been parted.
One of you has gone far away.
To you, I bid a fond farewell.
And a "Hello," to you, who stayed.

I'm now living with an incision
In place of one of you, breasts,
But I'm thankful I have my life…
And there's still one of you to caress!

THE METAMORPHOSIS

After my surgery, I realized some changes were needed in my life. Handling stress was the first task that required immediate attention. Then came a nutrition and exercise program. Finally, I knew I needed to be less critical of myself. This meant accepting and loving myself, if I was to be healthy in all aspects. This poem speaks to those changes.

The Metamorphosis

When confronted with life versus death,
It's life that I do choose.
I know there is so much more
Living that I want to do.

Yet, the shock of it all
Really set me on a path
Of examining my present life,
Rather than thinking of the aftermath.

My life is now changing.
With new eyes, I can see
That family, friends, and faith in God
Are what really matter to me!

I want to care for my body
In ways I have never done before,
And give myself time and permission
To minister to my needs more.

I'm trying to carefully monitor
All the foods that I eat,
Adding in the vitamins and minerals
That my body so desperately needs.

Exercise needs to be a part of each day;
It's something I always intended to do,
My mind and body really need it—
More, now, than I ever knew.

Meditation, relaxation, and stress reduction,
too,
Will now become my daily routine.
My worries need to be handled better,
To help my body stay pure and clean.

Life on this earth is really short,
And I want to live as long as I can.
Attitudes and living practices make a
difference,
As do loving and accepting myself as I am.

THE HEALING

Following my mastectomy, I felt the cancer had been totally removed and all I needed to do was "just recover" from my surgery. It was not a simple task, but I was sure I could manage it. I was looking forward to a normal life again.

This poem came from the feeling that I had been healed. It was written before chemotherapy had even been mentioned as a possible treatment.

What I find so interesting, now, is the fact that this poem speaks to the visualization image I used during my chemo treatments.

I speak of God's healing power as a "river of light."

The qualities of this river (i.e., warmth; goodness; and a white, translucent light) are the same ones that helped me focus on healing during my treatments.

Obviously, God was already at work within my heart when I wrote this poem. Only later did I become aware of His work in this way.

The Healing

Lord, Jesus,
Let your healing power
Flow through me
And remove
The impurities within.

Take away,
Dearest Jesus,
All the cancers that live
Within the corridors
Of my mind and body.

Your bright light,
White and translucent,
Sends warmth
And goodness flowing
Like a river inside me.

By Your power,
I am transformed,
From dark to light;
Shattered pieces to wholeness;
Death to life.

Love is present.
Fears are dissolved.
Filled with your light,

I am healed
And made whole again.

Sweet Jesus,
Your love,
Unconditional and pure,
Transcends all earthly desires
And renews my human vessel.

My Lord and Savior,
Thank you for the power
Of your healing touch,
And for a renewed life
That lets me see, with new eyes.

RELATIONSHIPS

Once I was diagnosed with cancer, my life seemed to fly before my eyes. I thought of all that I had (and had not) accomplished. I began to wonder about the meaning of life.

It occurred to me that such things as power, possessions, money, status, prestige, and how much one had collected meant absolutely nothing. I realized that, if I died today, little would really change. My family and friends would be touched with sadness. Perhaps, people at work would say something like, "She was a good person and it is too bad she is gone." But the truth was that nothing in this world would cease to exist, other than me. Life would continue for others, without my heart beating.

It came to my awareness that what counts are the relationships we have formed in our lives. They are my blessings and what is priceless. But they are also the things I take for granted.

I thought about love being the only reason we are on this earth and that we should be focused on spreading the love of Jesus Christ to all we encounter.

These thoughts brought forth this poem.

Relationships

Integrity and genuineness is
In all I think and do.
There's no place for deceit,
If, to myself, I'm true.

A positive outlook and focus,
I strive to maintain.
Hugs, laughter, and a sense of humor
Help to keep me sane.

Communicating feelings,
Sharing hopes and dreams,
And loving each other fully
Is what a relationship means.

Prestige, status, and power
Are not meaningful to me;
How I relate to my fellow man
Is the Jesus I hope others see.

To love others and to tell them
How much I truly care
Means living life to its fullest,
Taking risks, and being willing to share.

There are new lessons to learn
Each day that I live.
Being with people is vital,
And, to receive, I must give.

Life holds a special sweetness

That I treasure every day.
A true gift from God,
Loving others is the only way.

KIM, MY FRIEND

Throughout all the trials (the surgery and chemotherapy), my friend, Kim, was beside me.

She always had a word of encouragement to keep me going. I was forever grateful for her presence.

I knew God had blessed me abundantly with her friendship, but I still wondered what I could do to repay her for all of the support and assistance. She didn't expect something in return because she was my friend and I knew she loved me unconditionally. Nonetheless, I wanted to do something.

So, one day I sat down and wrote this poem. I was filled with the Holy Spirit when writing it and the words just flowed easily.

I gave Kim this poem along with another hematite cross that I had purchased especially for her.

Kim, My friend

Kim,
My friend,
You provide me with love
By your presence,
Your caring, and your concern.

Strength,
You share,
Through tears and smiles,
And by talking,
As well as the silent glances.

Loving
One another
Is so easy to do,
When I use you
As my example of how to be.

Faith
In God
Is a bond we share,
For we both know
That He heals through prayer.

A lesson
I am learning
From your experience
Is that healing is possible
In the presence of love.

Thankfulness,
I feel,
When I think of you,
And how important
You are in my life.

God
Has blessed me
With your friendship,

And He helps me to see
The Jesus that is present in you!

Our lives,
I know,
Will always be entwined,
Whether on this earth,
Or in heaven, when that day comes.

This cross,
Is my way
Of thanking Him, for you,
And of saying
That I love you, too!

"OH, MR. TENTMAKER"

Ruth, an elderly friend of mine in Michigan, sent this story to me one day. She knew I was desperately struggling and thought I would find solace and comfort by reading it. I was particularly touched when she shared that she used it herself when she was feeling down and weak.

Ruth was one of those people who had a very strong faith in the Lord and always appeared to handle adversity with such grace. She was a wonderful role model.

I felt very blessed by her candor, love, and willingness to share this marvelous story of the "Tentmaker."

"Oh, Mr. Tentmaker"
By Roselyn Aronson Staples

It was nice living in this tent when it was strong and secure and the sun was shining and the air was warm.

But, Mr. Tentmaker, it's scary now.

My tent is acting like it's not going to hold together. The poles seem weak and they shift with the wind. A couple of stakes have wiggled loose from the sand, and the worst of all, the canvas has a rip. It no longer

255

protects me from beating rain or stinging flies.

It's scary in here, Mr. Tentmaker. Last week, I was sent to the repair shop and some repairmen tried to patch the rip in my canvas. It didn't help much though, because the patch pulled away from the edges and now the tear is worse.

What troubled me most, Mr. Tentmaker, is that the repairmen didn't seem to notice that I was still in the tent. They just worked on the canvas while I shivered inside. I cried out once, but no one heard me.

I guess my real question is this: "Why did you give me such a flimsy tent? I can see by looking around the campground that some of the tents are much stronger and more stable than mine. Why, Mr. Tentmaker, did you pick a tent of such poor quality for me and even more important, what do you intend me to do about it?"

"Oh, little tent dweller, as the Creator and Provider of tents, I know all about you and your tent and I love you both.

"I made the tent for myself once and lived in it on your campground. My tent was vulnerable, too, and some vicious attackers ripped it to pieces while I was still in it. It was a terrible experience, but you'll be glad to know they couldn't hurt me. In fact, the whole occurrence was a tremendous advantage because it is this very victory over my enemy that frees me to be of present help to you.

"Little tent dweller, I am now prepared to come and live in your tent with you, *if you will invite me*. You will learn, as we dwell together, that real security comes from my being in your tent with you. When the storms come, you can bundle in my arms and I'll hold you. When the canvas rips, we'll go to the repair shop together.

"Someday, little tent dweller, your tent will collapse, for I've only designed it for temporary use. When it does, you and I will leave together. (I promise not to leave before you do.) Then, free of all that hinders or restricts, we will move to our permanent home and together, forever rejoice, and be glad."

THE FATHER IS VERY FOND OF ME

During many days of chemotherapy, I struggled to do much of anything. I thought I would never see another "normal" day in my life.

At times, I even wondered if I would ever live to see the actual termination of the chemo, as it felt like it was going on forever.

On one of those low days, another friend shared this verse with me, to give me comfort. It made a big difference!

The Father Is Very Fond Of Me

Perhaps our deepest act of faith is to believe that we have His heart, His power to love.

The deepest act of faith is not in the reality that God exists, but in the reality that He loves me, knows me by name, and that I have the power of His heart, His compassion within myself. But I will never discover this unless I exercise it. Select a person who is in and out of your life and decide to love Him. Christian love does not consist in finding an object who draws love from you. Christian friendship is not an accident of finding the right chemistry. Christian love is deliberate, it is chosen. I love this person not because He is worthy of my love, but because I have the capacity to love and to call to life, to create. No one of us will ever appreciate the power we have to give life to one another. We are the image of God because we have the power to believe in someone. We have the power to create life in Him. There is no greater gift which we can give to another person than our time, our presence. Every person has a capacity to bring us into a new room within ourselves, which has never been opened before. Every person comes to us with a key to a locked room, which we will never find without them. Each one of us is capable of being actualized by every person who enters into our lives in a unique way because each one has the capacity to unfold to us that we are the image of God. Therefore, I ask you to select anyone and love that person by a sure act of will and faith. Each one of us creates vibrations in one another. Each one of us creates distance or closeness, by a word, sometimes without a word, by directing or opening up ourselves, we open up another person. If one sincerely admires someone, they will mysteriously begin to open themselves. We have so much unlimited potential, which we have not even begun to use. Our prayer gives us an unlimited potential, which we have not even begun to use. Our prayer gives an unlimited capacity to carry his presence, to open to one another to His presence. Probably the greatest anguish, suffering which people undergo is their ability to accept love.

Author Unknown

DEAR DR. GILLIAM

After my surgery, when I was on the road to recovery, I decided I wanted to tell my doctor how much I appreciated having had him for my surgeon. I felt that I had been blessed by his presence and that he, indeed, had been another special gift from God.

I wrote this poem and shared it with him during one of my follow-up visits. I was very touched when he read it and then wiped a tear from his eye. We hugged one another and I knew then that I had done the right thing in sharing it.

Dear Dr. Gilliam

Dear Dr. Gilliam,
You are a kind and gentle man.
I love your warm smile
And your fine surgical hand.

From the very beginning.
I could see in your eyes
That your honesty and sincerity
Was something you didn't disguise.

You weren't afraid to listen
To the feelings that I shared,
And even when I cried,
Your touch showed me you cared.
I've enjoyed our little talks

And the stories that we've told—
Even a dream analysis, one day,
When I was feeling very bold.

I hope my surgical events
Have come to an abrupt end.
For I don't want you as a surgeon,
But I'd like you as my friend.

In conclusion, I must say
I really have been blessed,
For when God lead me to you,
He knew you were the best!

Thank you for being you!

MY HEAVENLY FATHER

I attended a day-long religious retreat in which we were asked to explore our relationship with God and to evaluate where we were in the process of growing closer to Him. One of the exercises requested the participants to write a brief letter to our heavenly Father, accepting the love that He offers.

Having successfully emerged from my surgery and chemotherapy, I was definitely feeling very thankful and grateful to my Lord and Savior. I wanted to tell Him how I felt. Although it is usually easier for me to compose a letter, this time, I found a poem expressed my feelings better.

My Heavenly Father

I accept all the love you offer,
Though I find it hard to understand.
How you can love me so,
When I am just a mortal woman?

I know you are always there for me;
All I have to do is come,
And you will fill me with your love,

263

Until you and I are one.

I want to receive all Your love,
And to feel Your spirit anew,
So I can be an instrument of peace
And rejoice in a love that's pure.

THE FINAL ACT OF LOVE

Putting my little Goldie to sleep was one of the most difficult tasks I have ever had to do. The fact that she had been with me longer than the time I lived with my parents was not something to take lightly.

I was torn between wanting to do the right thing and not causing her pain. It was not an easy decision, but when the time came, I knew it had to be done. This poem was written through my tears that evening when I was in such agony over my loss.

The Final Act of Love

Dear Goldie,
Today had to be the day.
I just couldn't see you suffer anymore.

Your pain
Had taken over your life,
Each day more miserable than the one before.

"It's okay,
You can go", I said.
And I hoped God would take you home.

But then,
When it didn't happen,
I knew I'd have to make that decision.

265

I agonized.
I didn't want to do it,
But your quality of life was slipping away.

Saturday's walk
Convinced me it was time,
For walking no longer brought you joy.

I tried
To deny the thought of it,
Because my heart was heavy with pain.

I had
To do it right away,
Because I had delayed it for too long.

The assistance
From Jim and Joann
Gave me strength to carry out the plan.

The drive
To the clinic was so painful,
I thought I really couldn't make it.

Your eyes
Looked at me with love
As I held you close to my heart.

I think
You understood it all,
And accepted it as the final act of love.
I cried
As he gave you the tranquilizer,

And I held you, until you were fully relaxed.

And then
I kissed you goodbye,
Left the room, and waited for it to be done.

You died
Instantly and peacefully,
And then, I knew you were home, with
Jesus.

Saying goodbye
To you today, Goldie,
Was also seeing a part of myself die, too.

I'm filled
With such love for you,
And I appreciate the treasure you have
been.

The memories
Of our time together
Will always be precious and cherished ones.

God gave
A special gift to me
By blessing my life with you, Goldie!

I love and miss you, baby girl!

GOODBYE, LITTLE GOLDIE

Five days after putting Goldie to sleep, I was scheduled to attend the "Walk to Emmaus." This was something I had been eagerly anticipating for several months, but suddenly I found myself wishing I didn't have to go. Friends told me that it was the best place to be. I thought they were saying that only because it would keep my mind occupied, thus preventing me from feeling sad about Goldie's death. My heart was so heavy with grief.

During that first evening, I had a difficult time trying to get involved in the program. I felt numb, distant, preoccupied, and inordinately sad. I didn't feel like talking to anyone, even though I went through the motions. All I really wanted to do was cry. Several times throughout the evening, it took all of my effort to prevent myself from openly sobbing.

Finally, I asked one of the pastors who was a support to the group to pray with me about my dogs. I'm not sure he really understood the nature of my concern, but we prayed together. After that point, the burden in my heart lifted. Of course, the sadness did not disappear, but I was more able to handle it.

Later in the evening, when there was a break, I pulled out a piece of paper and began writing this poem. Only then was I filled with a sense of peace.

Goodbye, Little Goldie

My sweet, little baby girl,
My heart grieves for you so.
The house is now empty,
Without your special glow.

Murdoch seems lost, too.
He's sullen and so down.
I think he's truly puzzled
As to where you have gone.

You were such a treasure
Of unconditional love so pure.
I really wonder just how I can live
With this heartache I can't cure.

I know you are with Jesus,
Which brings me great relief.
It brings peace to my heart
And helps to soothe the grief.

Daddy and Munchies are there, too.
I know they love you much.
I'm comforted that you are together,
Enjoying God's loving touch.

Someday, I'll join you all again,
Whenever that day will be.
Until then, I know you're surrounded

By His love, which sets you free.

THE EMMAUS WALK

During the Emmaus Walk weekend, I was filled to the point of overflowing with the Holy Spirit. I was surrounded with the love of God so much that, many times, all I could do was cry with joy and gratitude. The feelings were truly overwhelming and beyond wonderful!

I never stopped writing the entire weekend. It seemed that once I finished the poem on Goldie, I started another on the meaning the weekend. Each evening, although I was totally exhausted from the day's events, I stayed up long after others had fallen asleep, just to write my thoughts. By the end of the weekend, I had written two poems about my experiences with the "Walk to Emmaus."

The Emmaus Walk

Throughout this spirit filled weekend,
I have really been very touched
By the Christian love and actions of others;
It has meant so very much.

I have felt His Holy Presence
Move among us each and every day,
For He has been working His wonders

In, oh, so many different ways.

I know He wants us to love Him,
And be used as instruments in His plan,
For when we follow Him in faith,
He helps us to do all we can!

He is standing there now for us;
His arms are opened wide.
If we just turn to greet Him
All our needs, He will provide.

His love is so abundant;
It's unconditional and so pure.
It's wonderfully overwhelming,
And it's there for us, I'm sure.

There is joy in my being,
And contentment in my soul.
God's love surely does surround me,
And I feel truly whole.

As I leave this walk today,
I am filled with His radiant light.
I really want to be an example for Jesus,
For being in His presence is so right.

MY CHILD, FOR THE LOVE OF GOD

The Emmaus Walk weekend was one of being surrounded in total unconditional love. I am not sure that I have ever had such an experience before on this earth! When the 3½ days were over, I didn't want to leave. It truly was one of those "mountain top" experiences. I felt as though I had been given a glimpse of what heaven will be like and it was hard to return to the daily grind of this world. At the end of the weekend, it became clear why my friends had encouraged me to attend. Even though I had such a horrible beginning, it was a very comforting and healing weekend. The experience did not take away my grief, but carried me through it.

I viewed the weekend as a tribute and honor to the love that Goldie had shared with me for so many years. After that weekend, I was even more convinced that heaven is also for our beloved pets!!!

My Child, for the Love of God

He reaches out to me,
And softly calls my name.

Then He gently reminds me,
"My child, it's you I want to claim!"

His arms are open wide,
And He beckons me to come.
While He whispers in my ear,
"My Child, we can be one."

His love is there to give,
Surprisingly, just because I am.
But then He also asks of me,
"My child, please do all you can."

He takes my troubles and burdens,
As I lay them all before Him.
Then He easily assures me,
"My child, your sins are forgiven."

He wants to be my Lord and Savior
And have me yield my heart.
But He gently reveals to me,
"My child, first, you must start."

He pulls me close to Him,
And sweetly kisses my brow.
Then He whispers to me softly,
"My child, the time is now."

So, the test of wills has begun,

And He patiently waits to see.
But He strongly encourages,
"My child, please come to me."

A TRIBUTE TO OUR "TRISHA"

My friend, Trisha, was one of the first people to offer assistance when she learned what I was facing.

She drove down from Michigan to care for me and my dogs while I had my mastectomy. She never asked if she could do this; she just made the plans and carried them out. Our friendship was a special blessing from God and I was so fortunate to spend this time together with her.

Sadly, Trisha passed away, suddenly, on her 40th wedding anniversary, just a couple of years later.

A Tribute to Our "Trisha"

She was young in heart and mind,
Brimming full of smiles, laughter, and fun.
Each day brought a zest for living
That was contagious with those around her.
"Lord, she was your joyful servant!"

Her love of our Lord was strong and true,
Apparent both to family and friends.
It was important to be like Jesus,
And to live your will in all she would do.
"Lord, she was your faithful servant."

She gave of herself daily in so many ways,

Always ready to provide a helping hand.
Serving, consulting, singing, running errands,
Offering a listening ear to another.
"Lord, she was your humble servant."

Her sense of style was most unique,
With a love of colors that was just right.
Her jewelry was always the final touch,
To make a statement of who she was.
"Lord, she was your amazing servant."

She was the best of friends—
Patient, kind, compassionate, and true.
Eagerly coming to one's side to help,
Whenever there was a need for assistance.
"Lord, she was your willing servant."

Devotion to family was high on her list,
Beginning with her mighty love for Earl,
Followed then with each of her kids,
And adding the special gift of her grandchildren.
"Lord, she was your loving servant."

Now, Lord, You have called her home.
It is hard to understand why now,
But we know she now sits at your side,
And will be with you forevermore.
"Lord, she was your obedient servant."

Our hearts are heavy with her loss,
Because we miss and love her so.

We know you will take care of our Trisha,
For she is Your loving and precious child.
"Lord, we are your grateful and thankful
servants."

Trisha, I love you and thank God for the
time we had together.

Some of My Artwork

Painting #1

This painting represents my feelings when I was told I had breast cancer. I felt like I had been hit by a Mack truck. I was in shock and didn't want to accept the news. Unfortunately, the reality was clear. I had cancer and there was no turning back! My journey had begun!

Painting #2

The shock I felt from being told I had cancer was nothing compared to my reaction when chemotherapy was recommended. I felt that Mack truck had come back to hit me again. This painting represents the darkness that surrounded me because all I could see was black! I felt defeated!

Painting #3

I named this painting "In the Fire." It represents how I felt as I was in the midst of my chemo. Although I felt I was lost in a valley of darkness, what emerged was this painting of being in a fire.

Painting #4

This painting-collage speaks to the mix of feelings I experienced once my breast was removed. I struggled with body image because I knew I was broken. My earthly tent was damaged! The surgery sent me into a tailspin about how I would be viewed. I wanted people to look beyond my surface, but at the same time, I knew I had to redefine my view of self. My metamorphosis is symbolized by the butterflies.

Painting #5

This painting-collage was a reminder that I needed to rest in God, to be still and know God.

Painting #6

Once I accepted that God was in control, I knew He would provide for my needs and my healing. I rested in His provision and finally surrendered to Him. Only then was I able to feel His healing power working in my body. This painting documents the moment of surrender.

Painting #7

This painting represents the healing process that was taking place in my body. My cancer was being healed. More importantly, it was my hardened heart that received healing, too. There is always a holy surprise when Jesus is involved! This was mine!

Painting #8

When one is going through a trial, you have to have hope. It becomes a light on which you can focus when you are in the darkness. That is what this painting-collage provided me.

About the Author

Rita Carbuhn (1945-) was born in Iowa, where her early years were spent on a farm. It was from this beginning and her German ancestry that she learned the importance of self-sufficiency. This lesson would become a central part of her coping skills as she matured. After the farm was sold, her family moved to Atlantic, Iowa, where they lived for the next six years. During this time, Rita learned how to play the clarinet and was part of the school band. Due to her father's ill health, the family moved to Florida just as she entered high school. Again, band was a major part of her school activities. She was a bright student and graduated in the top 1% of her class.

Rita was awarded a health career scholarship from the March of Dimes and was accepted into the nursing program at the University of Florida. While in school, she was a proud member of the Gator Band and traveled to many Bowl games because of that association. Rita subsequently earned a bachelor's degree in nursing. Although she had a job in community health nursing waiting for her in Orlando, it was at that point when she realized her life needed to take a different turn and changed her focus to psychiatric nursing. As a result, she took a job in the psychiatric unit at Shand's Teaching Hospital. She describes this decision as "finding my home." It was a decision she has never regretted. Within two years, she returned to school to obtain her Master's degree in psychiatric nursing.

When her graduate studies were completed, Rita moved to San Diego, California, and obtained a position with the County of San Diego Mental Health Services. While there, she worked as a staff nurse, a nursing supervisor, and then became the staff educator. In that role, she oriented all new staff (including mental health techs, nurses, medical students, and physicians) and was responsible for developing all education programs and seminars for the facility.

Two-and-a-half years later, she moved to Michigan to get married. When plans for the marriage fell through, she decided to settle in Michigan anyway and worked in a variety of mental health administrative roles at one of the hospitals there.

After 22 years of working in the hospital and surviving a series of reorganizations and changes at work, she realized it was time for her to leave. In very short order, she was offered a position in Kentucky and felt "called" to accept. She held great expectations for the move since she believed it was orchestrated by God. However, it was shortly after her move to Kentucky that she was diagnosed with breast cancer. This event dramatically altered her life. More importantly, it changed her relationship with Jesus. She learned how to rely on Him and be aware of His presence on a daily basis. The early lessons of self-sufficiency were ultimately transformed into ones of surrender and reliance on the Lord. Surprisingly, her expectations for the move were met, but in a spiritual way. The outcome was a more intimate relationship with her Lord and Savior, Jesus.

After her ordeal with breast cancer, she relocated to Tulsa, Oklahoma, where she worked in two different psychiatric facilities in administrative roles for several years before moving into a teaching role. Currently, she teaches mental health nursing at Tulsa Community College and describes this position as her "pre-retirement" job. She loves teaching and particularly enjoys being able to share her fifty years of experience with her students. She says teaching is "energizing, fun, and keeps me young." There are no plans for retirement in the near future.

Rita enjoys many creative activities, including cooking, gardening, interior decorating, scrapbooking, and all kinds of art (watercolor, acrylic, and mixed media). She is now comfortable in defining herself as an artist! Some of her artwork can been seen in her first book, *Signs of His Light: My Spiritual Journey with Cancer*, along with several of her poems, as both forms of art served as her therapy during her journey.

Rita no longer plays the clarinet, but enjoys listening to contemporary Christian artists. Her dogs have replaced the role (and void) of children, so they hold a very dear place in her heart. Her current love is a 15-year-old, "very spoiled" Bichon. Traveling became a passion many years ago so she has visited 49 of our 50 states (only Hawaii remains). Italy and Israel are her favorite countries, but she has also been to Canada, Mexico, Turkey, France, Europe, and Brazil. She says, "I love learning about other cultures," so her desire is to travel to as many countries as possible.

Becoming an author (and sharing with others her life experiences and lessons learned) has been a long-standing dream—one she is happy she made a reality! She has plans to publish a book of poetry as well as a book of true short stories about the antics of the fur-babies she has had over the years.

NOTE:

If you want to connect with Rita, email her at rcarbuhn@cox.net or find her on Facebook at https://www.facebook.com/rita.carbuhn.3 and let her know you read her book!

48671145R00161

Made in the USA
Middletown, DE
19 June 2019